Symbol and Substance in Japanese Lacquer

Symbol and Substance in Japanese Lacquer

LACQUER BOXES FROM THE COLLECTION OF ELAINE EHRENKRANZ

BY BARBRA TERI OKADA

WEATHERHILL
New York • Tokyo

First edition, 1995

©1995 by Barbra Teri Okada
Photographs by Dan Loffler

Published by Weatherhill, Inc.
568 Broadway, Suite 705, New York, NY 10012
Protected by copyright under the terms of the
International Copyright Union; all rights reserved.

Printed in Hong Kong

Library of Congress Cataloging in Publication Data

Okada, Barbra Teri.
      Symbol and substance in Japanese lacquer: lacquer
boxes from the collection of Elaine Ehrenkranz / by
Barbra Teri Okada.
            p.   cm.
      Includes bibliographical references and index.
      ISBN 0-8348-0321-6 (hard)
      1. Lacquer boxes—Japan—Exhibitions.
   2. Ehrenkranz, Elaine—Art collections—Exhibitions.
   3. Lacquer boxes—Private collections—United States
—Exhibitions. I. Title.
   NK9900. 7. J3039 1995
   745.7'26'09520747471—dc20   95-11236
                                                      CIP

Contents

Foreword

I have a passion for Japanese lacquer. During the time I was assembling the collection of Japanese lacquer boxes represented in the catalogue *A Sprinkling of Gold*, I searched for fine examples from all periods that represented different functions, styles, techniques, and aesthetics. My goal was to form a well-balanced collection, one that reflected my taste. That about a third of the collection was produced before the nineteenth century, with one piece dating back to the early sixteenth century, signifies that without my conscious awareness, I had become deeply involved in this genre.

Many of the qualities found in early lacquer are particularly appealing to me. Subjects from nature are rendered with subtlety and elegant simplicity. Effects of delicate refinement and sophistication are often achieved with as few as two or three basic techniques from the myriad of techniques available to the *maki-e shi*. In addition to these attributes, lacquer with the feeling and appearance of age, and a concurrent sense of history, has always held a special fascination for me.

After the publication of *A Sprinkling of Gold* in 1983, I was inspired to further pursue my interest in Japanese lacquer boxes by collecting the earliest pre-nineteenth-century examples I could find. Not only had such boxes become hard to find, but once found, proved difficult to research. I discovered there was little descriptive information in English relating to the function, techniques, and dating of these boxes. Because of the dearth of such information, I became acutely aware of the need for a book exploring these subjects, which would be invaluable to scholars, collectors, and students of Japanese art. I then decided to invite Barbra Teri Okada to write a comparative, in-depth study on pre-nineteenth-century Japanese lacquer, using my boxes as the basis for her research. I was delighted that she agreed to accept the challenge. It has been an exciting joint effort, with my role being to find early boxes appropriate to a study of this nature.

The search has led me down the most challenging and exhilarating path of my collecting experience. I had been lulled into a sense of security by my fortuitous success in finding early boxes for my first collection. In forming the second, I found it increasingly difficult to discover good examples of such pieces. It was virtually impossible to acquire boxes from the Heian, Kamakura, and early Muromachi periods, and certainly nothing earlier. Many of these boxes had been destroyed in fires and earthquakes, and most of those that had survived were housed in museums and private collections. However, through perseverance and good fortune, I was able to find interesting examples from the late Muromachi, Momoyama, and early-to mid-Edo periods. I should mention that there were a few fine boxes I had to forego due to escalating prices. An increased awareness and interest among collectors in early lacquers, along with their scarcity, was partly responsible for this price surge. This made me even more appreciative of the early boxes of high quality that I was fortunate enough to have already acquired.

Though every box added to the collection gave me great pleasure, there were a few acquisitions that gave me an indefinable sense of accomplishment. An exquisite writing box, decorated with an open fan (entry 30) was being auctioned at Christie's in New York. Although the estimate was realistic, I feared that the actual sales price would be way beyond my reach, due to the fine quality of the box and the cachet of its provenance (Red Cross Loan Exhibition of Japanese Art, 1915). As it turned out, my fears were unfounded, and for some reason I was able to acquire it for even less than I had anticipated.

Not as exhilarating as this auction fever, but equally gratifying, was my acquisition of two very early and fine boxes (see entries 28 and 35). There was a dealer's exhibition at a *netsuke* convention that displayed what seemed to be hundreds of lacquer boxes. I spotted two unusual examples on a bottom shelf, that at a glance, appeared to be early. In my haste to see all the dealers' displays in the short time I had, I forged ahead. A few minutes later, anxiety began to mount as I realized I might be missing a great collecting opportunity. I rushed back, and much to my relief, the boxes were still there! As it turned out, further study proved both boxes to be a collector's dream—not only fine examples from early periods, but rare as well.

In forming this collection, I was most fortunate to have the support and help of many people. First, I wish to express my deep appreciation to Barbra Teri Okada, who again accepted the challenge of writing a book based on my collection. She has taken many trips to Japan in order to do original research that could not have been accomplished anywhere else. This research entailed translations from Japanese texts, study of museum collections of early lacquer, and consultation with Japanese experts in the field. With her extensive knowledge and expert eye, Ms. Okada was able to provide me with immeasurable assistance in my final selection.

I want to express particular thanks to Michael Dean, a London dealer and highly respected collector of Japanese lacquer, who provided me with a large number of the boxes that appear in this publication. His exquisite taste, scholarship, and special interest in early Japanese lacquer proved invaluable to the formation of my collection.

I am very grateful to Dan Loffler for his exceptional skill and professionalism in photographing my collection. He displayed unlimited patience in his willingness to photograph a box as often as necessary to achieve the fine results seen in this book.

I am especially grateful to my husband, Joel, for cheering me on. I recall intense discussions weighing the pros and cons of forming a second collection while on long summer walks in the woods of Maine. Not only did he encourage me to undertake this venture, but continued to inspire me when my spirits flagged. He always advised me to trust my judgment. I usually did, and have not had cause to regret it.

I hope that the information in this book will excite and encourage enthusiasts of Japanese lacquer to further explore this complex and fascinating subject. It would give me great satisfaction to think that the research difficulties I encountered will be eased somewhat for future collectors and scholars. As for my collection, I would feel well-rewarded if my lacquer boxes were widely viewed, thereby inspiring in others some of the passion I have felt for this remarkable art form.

Elaine Ehrenkranz

Acknowledgments

In the more than thirty-five years I have studied Japanese art, I have been most fortunate in meeting the right people at the right time. It is impossible to express my appreciation to all of them here, but I would like to highlight a few, for without them I would never have been able to pursue my studies or complete this book.

To the Reverend Hozen Seki of the Nishi Honganji sect at the New York Buddhist Temple, I owe my first formal training in the field of Buddhism, in Japanese painting techniques, and in the "consciousness" of Japanese art. His hand guided me in these areas for more than a decade. In 1972 I met Charles A. Greenfield, whose personal collection included some of the finest examples of lacquer in the world. He taught me for more than twelve years, during which time he gave me free access to his collection and library.

In 1973 I went to Japan for the first time, and stayed at the home of the Reverend Kakusho Imakoji of the Nishi Honganji. He and his family, especially his daughter Yūko, with whom I became fast friends, have been a haven in Japan for me for more than twenty years, and have introduced me to art treasures in private hands that I would never have seen otherwise. A few words of thanks here can never express my heartfelt love and appreciation for their perpetual hospitality.

While staying at the Imakoji house I met Emiko Takeda and her family, and through Emiko I met my lacquer teacher, the artist Mizuuchi Kyohei, a superb artisan as well as a warm and patient educator.

Over sixteen years ago I had the good fortune to meet my dear friend Reiko Suzuki and her husband Hideo in New York, just before their return to Tokyo. Without Reiko's assistance I would never have been able to learn very much about lacquer in Japan. Her unremitting willingness to help and give of her time, along with her remarkable translation abilities, matched my own desire to trace sources of information, regardless of the time and effort required.

The chief of cultural affairs of the *Nihon Keizai Shimbun*, Kunio Miyata, and his assistant at the time, Katsumi Suzuki, have helped me in ways too numerous to mention over the last fourteen years, and it was through their auspices that I was able to meet the famous National Treasure of the lacquer arts, Matsuda Gonroku. His student, Yoshikuni Taguchi, a well-known teacher in his own right, in turn allowed me to visit the lacquer department at the Tokyo University of Fine Arts and Music.

To Hirokazu Arakawa, retired curator of the lacquer collection at the Tokyo National Museum, I owe a debt starting almost seventeen years ago. He patiently and generously allowed me to examine the lacquer boxes in the museum collection and trained my eye in a manner impossible without his severe guidance.

Twenty years ago I met Yasuhiro Nishioka, now the world's leading expert on Chinese lacquer and chief curator of the department of oriental antiquities at the Tokyo National Museum. Under his influence, I have recently begun to reevaluate the influence of China on seventeenth- and eighteenth-century Japanese lacquers. He has been a good friend and very supportive of my struggles in the field.

To Hachirō Ōuchi, president of the Fujii Urushi Kogei Company, one of the few remaining *urushiya* in the Tokyo area, I owe my firsthand experience of the process of lacquer refining, as well as the photographs which appear in the introduction.

To Elaine Ehrenkranz, friend, artist, and collector, thank you for the second opportunity to publish another part of your lacquer collection. Elaine is one of the few collectors more interested in education than ego, and it has always been a pleasure to work with her.

Finally, thanks to my ever-encouraging husband David, who, when he could, read and corrected some of the material that went into this book. Thanks also to my long-suffering typist Annette Phillips (who had to adjust to a word processor); to Naoko Yaegashi, my old helper who faithfully came to my aid again; to Allen Campbell for his editorial contributions; and to my countless associates and friends, who were always encouraging. To David Noble, my editor, and to Ray Furse and the whole crew at Weatherhill, I can only say that it has been a long road, but it has ended well.

Last, but certainly not least, my thanks go to my dear friend and editor extraordinaire—Dr. Frederick Baekeland. Without his generosity with his time, talent, and disciplined mind, I know this book would not have been published. I alone, however, bear responsibility for any errors.

Opposite page: detail of the lid of a mirror box (kagamibako) showing the lacquer techniques of e-nashiji, kakiwari, and gold fundame. Overleaf: the complete box, showing its design of two flowering cherry trees against a hillside. Momoyama period, late 16th to early 17th century. Dimensions: DIA *5⅜ x* H *2½ in (13.7 x 6.4 cm)*

Introduction:
Lacquer as a Substance and Artistic Medium

The word "lacquer" derives from *lak*, the name ancient Persians gave to a resinous substance secreted by certain insects. In common usage in the West, "lacquer" has continued to be considered nearly synonymous with shellac, i.e., a varnish formed by suspending resin in a solvent such as alcohol. This type of "lacquer" dries by evaporation, leaving a hard and shiny surface, but one that can be marred by most liquids and destroyed by a wide range of solvents.

In contrast, Japanese lacquer, or *urushi*, is derived from the nonresinous sap of the *Rhus verniciflua* tree, a member of the Anacardiaceae family, which includes poison oak, poison ivy, and poison sumac. Its highly allergenic properties pose a problem for the artisans who use it in their work. Contact with *urushi* causes a reaction resembling a serious case of poison oak poisoning, and if inhaled, the vapor may cause extensive internal damage. Although varieties of the tree are widely distributed through Asia, the trees that yield the best quality *urushi* are to be found in Japan, where it has served as a major vehicle for artistic expression for more than fifteen hundred years. (In fact, lacquered objects have been found in ancient burial mounds dating back as far as the early Jomon period, 4000–3000 BC.)

Japanese lacquer does not dry; it hardens through a process of polymerization. Once rigid, it remains impregnable to most solvents, except for strong reagents such as sulfuric or hydrochloric acid, though it can be damaged by direct sunlight after prolonged exposure. Its remarkable adhesive properties and insolubility in water make *urushi* an extremely durable binding agent. In addition to its role in the production of fine lacquerwork such as the pieces introduced in this book, *urushi* is the major adhesive employed in the restoration of Japanese wood sculpture, is used in the repair of pottery and porcelains, and serves as the glue used to bind gold leaf to thread in the making of textiles.

The unique characteristics of this substance are explained by its chemical composition: 10–35 percent water, small amounts of albumen and gum arabic, and about 60–80 percent urushiol, a pyrocatechol. At moderate temperatures and high humidities (ideally 75–85 degrees Fahrenheit and a relative humidity of about eighty percent), in combination with the enzyme laccase found in the albumen, urushiol undergoes a cross-linked polymerization reaction that causes it to harden.[1] (Although this process is actually one of hardening or curing, it is commonly referred to as "drying," a convention also adopted in this book.) Thus one may look upon *urushi* as "the most ancient industrial plastic known to man."[2]

In order to insure complete hardening when it is applied to a surface, thin layers must be carefully built up. Too thick an application may result in wrinkling as a consequence of uneven exposure to the humid atmosphere. After about twenty-four hours, the surface to which the *urushi* has been applied may feel dry, but it takes much longer for the chemical reaction to reach completion. During this phase the fumes released are still volatile enough to poison those who have not become desensitized, as refining does not remove the poisonous qualities of this sap.

The Lacquer Tree and Its Harvest

The lacquer tree (*urushi no ki*) blossoms in May and early June with small yellowish-green flowers; the sap oozes naturally from the tree from mid-June through late October, and it is during this period that harvesting of *urushi* typically takes place. Ideally the tree should be at least ten years old (although some say only four) and the trunk at least ten centimeters in diameter before it is tapped. The sap runs in a channel between the outer bark and the growing layer of the inner wood core. Small incisions are cut to mark the place for deeper incisions to follow, beginning about twenty centimeters from the ground and continuing at intervals of forty centimeters, for up to four more successive markings. The short, forked knife used for both marking and main incisions is called a *kakigama*.

The first cuts, called *metate*, are not made to gather the *urushi*, but only to show the main cutter where he must start the incisions that will penetrate the bark. As many as ten markings per tree per session are made. There is repeated harvesting during the season, with fresh cuts added below the older ones, so that there are sets of incisions (fig. 1). To protect the tree from shock, the deeper incisions are made only once every five days. A curved spatular instrument called a *kakihera* (fig. 2) is used to scoop away the translucent, grayish matter that is exuded at the surface of the cut. The collected *urushi* is scraped against the lips of small wooden cups that are then emptied into wooden buckets. As exposure to light and air has an almost immediate physical effect on the collected material, it is essential to work efficiently. Each incision produces about one gram of the substance and each tree can be tapped for about 187 grams of *urushi* per season.

Depending on the local climate and the size of the tree, the best harvests are those from the middle of July through August, or through to the last harvest in autumn. Most trees will show perhaps four sets of incisions on either side by the end of October.

Different grades of lacquer are the result of variables such as the age of the tree, climatic conditions during its growth, what part of the tree the sap is taken from, and the part of season in which it is tapped. Although the *Rhus verniciflua* tree was supposedly introduced from either Korea or China about fifteen hundred years ago, the finest and most homogeneous lacquer comes from the middle part of the main trunk of a Japanese-grown lacquer tree. Chinese lacquer is considered inferior because its urushiol content is lower, and therefore its sap does not harden as well.

Nothing is wasted when the tree is tapped out. The nuts produced in the fall (fig. 3) contain a seed

fig. 1

fig. 2

fig. 3

fig. 4

from which a wax is extracted for the manufacture of candles, lipstick, and medicinal ointments. A polishing material that is used to help give silk a shine is also manufactured from this nut. The grain of the tree's core is yellow-green and so beautiful that it is often incorporated into the posts and flooring for the *tokonoma* area in the Japanese home.[3]

Presently Japan produces only about three percent of the nearly five hundred tons of *urushi* demanded annually by the Japanese lacquer industry, and trees are found only in the prefectures of Aomori, Aichi, Ibaraki, Nara, Kyoto, and Okayama. Of the small amount of *urushi* that is still gathered in Japan, the best is saved for the final surface work produced by *maki-e* artists. (*Maki-e*, literally, "sprinkled picture," is a uniquely Japanese decorative process in which colored or metallic powders are sprinkled on a design drawn in wet lacquer.) The rest of the country's lacquer is imported, mainly from China (about 90 percent), with smaller amounts of lower quality lacquer coming from Taiwan, Thailand, Vietnam, and Burma.

Today, nontoxic plastics can be used to replicate both the forms and designs of articles previously created with *urushi*. Their resemblance to real lacquerware can be remarkably deceptive; they are also cheaper, less toxic to manufacture, and less expensive for the purchaser. However, objects made using synthetics are typically for general household use. The majority of the surviving Japanese lacquer artists, who are a dying breed, seem to prefer the softer qualities and quiet magical luster of the natural material.

The Refining Process

After the sap has been transferred from the collection cups into wooden buckets, it is covered with glazed paper to avoid further exposure to contaminants such as dust and to light (fig. 4). Because *urushi* is extremely sensitive to ultraviolet rays, the underfluid darkens even during the short time it takes to transport it, and a thick milky film forms on the top. The containers are then taken to an *urushiya*[4] and poured into vats of varying sizes (fig. 5). This establishment is not only a refinery but also a warehouse, for its operator acts as a manufacturer, an importer, a wholesaler and a retailer. Such centralization is necessary because the sap is so poisonous that a person who is not desensitized could easily develop a toxic reaction by simply touching a wet stain or breathing in the fumes the liquid expels.

At the refinery, the first step in the elimination of impurities begins. Particles of wood, bark, and other solid impurities are filtered out by pouring the thick liquid through a piece of tightly woven fabric such as linen. The filtered substance is termed *seishi urushi* (purified *urushi*). The very best quality liquid, which comes from the middle of the trunk of the tree and is kept separate from the rest, is then further cleaned by a spin-filter system. This plain, specially purified *seishi urushi* is known as *ki shōmi urushi*. Pure, almost clear in appearance, this unprocessed substance is neither heated nor adulterated in any way, and is the highest grade of lacquer possible. It is retailed only for use by those artists who require it in the final coats of their work.

fig. 5

ALTERATION BY HEAT OR COLORING

"Cooked *urushi*" (*seisei urushi*) results from the processing of all Japanese lacquer that has not been set aside as *ki shōmi urushi*. (The best grades of imported lacquer may also be left unprocessed; however, these are still considered inferior to native material and therefore not classified as *ki shōmi urushi*.) During the processing, additives (*suki*) such as oil, light coloring materials, or the intense black (*kuro*) of iron filings are introduced by slow blending in large wooden vats. Warmth (*kurome*) gently applied by coiled heating elements suspended above the individual vats simulates the action of the sun, which was relied on in earlier times. Simultaneously, a mechanical blender slowly

fig. 6

fig. 7

fig. 8

mixes in the additives. This "cooking" process removes the excess water contained in the natural sap and guarantees uniform drying when the lacquer is later applied to a surface. When this process is complete, little water remains in the resulting viscous, grayish brown or black substance (fig. 6).

The blended lacquer is now ready for final purification by a spin-filter system that involves the use of cotton wool to attract and trap any remaining particles of impurities. The cotton wool is shredded gradually by hand into a small heated container of lacquer (fig. 7), while continuous application of dry heat sustains the liquid state of the lacquer.

The heated mixture of lacquer and shredded cotton is then placed in a cloth-lined metal-mesh basket which is spun in a centrifuge (fig. 8). After passing through the cloth lining of the basket, the filtered material flows into a large pail from an open tap at the base of the machine, which is also lined with a final filter (fig. 9).

CLASSIFICATIONS AND GRADES

The two major kinds of *urushi* are thus unprocessed and processed (or "cooked"). The processed *urushi* is then further subdivided into "plain" *urushi*—to which light coloring material, or oil, or both may be added—and "black" *urushi*—a dark, lower quality lacquer to which color in the form of iron filings or oil is added before cooking. Each type remains in its own storage tub either for further processing or for direct sale. There is a parallel classification of three standard grades as follows.

A-quality urushi is the specially purified, unprocessed *seishi urushi* known as *ki shōmi urushi*. It is used only for the pride of the Japanese lacquer artistry, *maki-e*.

B-quality urushi is "plain" processed *urushi* (*seisei urushi*), with or without the addition of oil or coloring matter. The most frequently used type of processed "plain" lacquer without oil involves the addition of a coloring agent known as gamboge (*shio*), a resin derived from the gum tree. This orange-to-brown coloring additive lends a yellowish tint to the lacquer. When used to suspend adulterated sprinkled gold in the popular background technique known as *nashiji* ("pear-skin ground"), the gamboge deepens the tone of the metal in suspension, thereby contriving the appearance of a more expensive material than actually used.

Processed "plain" lacquer with oil and color is combined with cinnabar, a pure red coloring matter, to make red lacquer, which is used in the many-layered, Chinese-derived technique known in Japanese as *tsuishu*. The oil lends a slight sheen to the multi-layered form.

C-quality urushi, black but without the addition of oil, is mainly used for the many undercoatings required in the preparation of the core of a lacquer object. A slightly thicker variant, combined with sawdust and rice paste, is utilized to form the sealant known as *kokuso*, used in the process of assembling lacquer boxes. The no-oil type of C-quality *urushi* may also be used for the black, waxy final ground of the *maki-e* technique known as *ro-iro*.

A somewhat glossier effect is achieved using oil-added black lacquer on a surface. As this is a less costly method of finishing, it is commonly used to coat the interiors of undecorated boxes or to finish less conspicuous surfaces such as the bottom a box or the underside of a tray.

Many more categories exist, but those described above are those most commonly stocked by present-day *urushiya*. There are only one hundred twenty *seisei urushiya* left in Japan, and only four in the Tokyo area.

Construction of the Form

The term "form" refers to the base or core that supplies the underlying shape of a lacquer object.[5] Its exceptionally complicated preparation is steeped in a

fig. 9

ritual that has remained virtually unchanged for over a thousand years.

The production of the form for a single piece of fine lacquerware calls for the extensive cooperation of a variety of skilled craftsmen. For the sake of brevity, only the procedures for creating the form for a box (as opposed to trays or other objects) will be described here.

SEASONING OF THE WOOD

Almost all lacquer boxes have a core of wood, the seasoning of which is critical to its durability. Traditionally, thorough seasoning required from twenty to fifty years, depending on the variety of wood and purpose for which it was to be employed. Because of this remarkable requirement, it was necessary for generations of related craftsmen to succeed each other, and a major part of a family's inheritance was, and still is, the previous inventory of drying wood stored in covered sheds or even in the family home.

Pine and cypress were considered the best woods for the construction of boxes. However, paulownia, cherry, zelkova, woven strips of bamboo (see entry 19), animal hide, and even paper were, and still are, used in shaping a core, though not necessarily in the case of art pieces. Before the Meiji period (1868–1912), it was almost unthinkable to skimp on the time required for proper seasoning of the wood, but during the third quarter of the nineteenth century increased demand from abroad spurred artisans to produce works of art more quickly. Less-skilled craftsmen grew careless and began using green or only partially-seasoned wood.

Excellent examples of the problems caused by this practice may be observed in many of the lacquers created by the great artist Shibata Zeshin (1808–91). Due to the constant demand for his extraordinary work, he formed an atelier that literally mass-produced his designs. As a result, within a short time after the completion of an object, ill-fortified corners sometimes separated from the central paneling to which they were joined. Some pieces warped after delivery abroad, and due to the use of "green" wood, many beautifully decorated lacquers were irreparably damaged by cracking. Although central heating and air-conditioning are often blamed for such changes in lacquer works imported to the West, properly prepared and lacquered wood should not continue to shrink, even when it resides in a country less humid than Japan.

CORNERING

Joining two pieces of wood to form a corner is performed by specialists who cut and fit all connecting sections. The construction of a joint may be curved or straight, and it is reinforced on the inside with a filler and sealant—typically *kokuso*, a combination of sawdust, rice paste, and black *urushi*. Until recently, the corners side panels for a box of top quality were assembled with either rabbet or dovetail joinery. The slim rectangular panels for the bottom and lid were usually joined by the tongue and groove method.

Before the twentieth century almost all Kyoto artisans and most other regional craftsmen used more expensive and time-consuming construction techniques than are employed today. Currently, with the exception of the highest quality lacquers, corners of boxes are now joined solely by mitering, reinforced only by a small piece of wood inserted on the inside of each corner, bound with *kokuso*.

LACQUER AS A BINDER AND SEALANT

The raw wood surface of the core will now receive meticulous attention through the many applications of undercoatings and various sealants necessary to establish a perfect surface for the various decorative *maki-e* techniques that will follow.

The process of applying lacquer is usually divided into three distinct stages—the primary coating or undercoating (*shitaji nuri*), the middle coating (*naka nuri*), and the final coating (*uwa nuri*)—all of which are performed, as described below, in separate ateliers that are manned by highly skilled and experienced craftsmen.

THE PRIMARY COATING (SHITAJI NURI)
Initial priming, in three stages, is completed by a small shop of four to six men. The seating position in the group reflects the seniority, based on experience, of its members.

The head craftsman who receives the formed box from the joiner is solely responsible for the initial inspection of each object. He carefully checks the box's components, front and back, and then proceeds to cut and fill the outside part of the joints with more *kokuso*, which helps to strengthen and further bind the junctions. Each box is then passed to the next workman, who will plane and sand the edges, to provide an even smoother surface for the next step. At this point the box is given a base coat of plain, low-quality black *urushi*.

Traditionally, at this stage in the production of the very highest-quality box, linen was pasted down onto all inner surfaces with black *urushi*, a procedure customary when neither time nor money was a consideration. This was especially true when objects were made to order for the shogunate or a member of the court or provincial aristocracy. However, during the Edo period (1600–1868) there was a dramatic increase in lacquer production due to an enormous demand from the rising middle class. This encouraged the substitution of speed for prudent and careful skill, leading to the abbreviation of the preliminary stages of preparation, as well as modification of the time-consuming procedures needed to smooth the surfaces of the raw material. Thus most lacquer boxes produced from the seventeenth century onward have received only a strip of fabric about four inches wide on their joined inner corners. As a result, fill work is necessary to completely level all the surfaces adjoining the areas covered in fabric. It is this method that the following description addresses.

After the linen is firmly glued to the corner areas, a thick mixture of rice paste and a claylike substance known as *jinoko* is blended with black *urushi* and applied to all the surfaces of the form as a sealant. The resultant rough surface is then ground to a smooth finish with sandpaper or a whetstone. *Jinoko* is added to the lacquer to absorb excess water and prolong the drying time of the lacquer (a benefit). *Jinoko*, a claylike material containing diatomaceous earth, with a porous, honeycomblike structure in its natural state, was discovered in the 1660s in the Wajima area of the Noto Peninsula in northern Honshū. Before it can be used, the substance must first be mixed with water, formed into stubby oval shapes, and baked in the sun on racks. The large, dry pellets are then covered with wood powder in alternating layers, one of pellets then one of wood powder. The whole mass is next set ablaze so that the large, oblong-shaped pellets are scorched black. After cooling, they are crushed by hand in a large mortar and pestle. The resultant powder is sifted and stored in three predetermined grades of coarseness, which are termed *ippenji* ("first ground"), *nihenji* ("second ground"), and *sambenji* ("third ground").

After the foundation of thick rice paste, *urushi*, and plain ungraded *jinoko* is applied, allowed to dry, and polished, three additional coats are then laid down, consisting of the above three grades of ground *jinoko* mixed with black *urushi*. They differ only in the degree of coarseness of the *jinoko*, and normally proceed from the coarsest to finest grade. Thus, the first coat is called *ippenji nuri* ("first ground coating," the word *nuri* meaning "coating" or, by extension, "lacquer"). This coarse coat is applied, first to the interior and then the exterior, let dry, and then polished with charcoal and water. The second and third ground coatings are added in turn, and all surfaces must be thoroughly dry before the next coat is applied. As most core work is performed in the highly humid area of Wajima on the Japan Sea, additional artificial humidity is seldom needed, especially in the summer months. The boxes and their lids are set on racks between each application, allowing all surfaces to be exposed to the humid air to facilitate the curing process.

At this point the materials added during joinery have been made indiscernible to the eye and to the touch. An absolutely even surface is required for the work that will follow. After a final inspection by the head of the shop to guarantee there is no visible variation in the level of all the surfaces, the form is now considered ready for the next stage.

THE MIDDLE COATINGS (NAKA NURI)

At the middle coating shop, the master carefully examines each piece. Although the base quality of the *urushi* used in this next stage of finishing is the same as that employed in stage one, further refinement is required, as it must be filtered through special paper one more time. The inside is coated with purified C-quality *urushi* and then placed in the humidifying chamber customarily used from this stage on.

Up to this point, the use of a special humidifying chamber, the *furo*, or wet box (an enclosed chamber with shelves and typically lined with moist rags) has probably not been necessary. But now the objects are sealed within it, where they are not only humidified but also kept from contamination by light and dust. The degree of humidity is controlled by the spraying of regulated amounts of moisture onto the hanging cloths that surround the interior. Because curing takes so long, and cold makes the consistency of lacquer difficult to handle even today, little core work is done in the winter months. However, mass manufacturing of lacquerware can be carried out at in any season, by utilizing a heated, automatic *furo*.

Depending on the season, the approximate curing time is about eight hours, after which the surface is polished with a whetstone and the piece passed on to another workman, who will lacquer the outside. If further examination reveals that the surface is not absolutely smooth, a thin mixture of powdered pumice, *urushi*, and a little water (the mixture called *sabi urushi*) is applied. After drying, it is again polished down, either with charcoal and water or a whetstone.

THE FINAL COATINGS (UWA NURI)

The final coats may be applied at the same shop, or the piece may be passed on to another group specializing in them. Both a higher grade of black *urushi* and further filtration is required at this stage. The lacquer is now squeezed through three sheets of a distinctive type of paper, then through five more combined sheets, and then again through seven pieces of this special filter, thereby guaranteeing absolute purity.

After the final polishing, the surfaces of both box and lid are carefully scrutinized for the slightest imperfection and only after such exacting examination does the shop release the box to a *maki-e* artist, who transforms the unadorned surfaces into magnificent objects like those that appear on the following pages.

THE EVOLUTION OF THE LACQUER ART AND ITS TECHNIQUES

Patronage of lacquer art in Japan began with the imperial court, which directly ruled the country during the Asuka (552–645), Nara (645–794), and Heian (794–1185) periods. With the emergence into power and de facto rule of the samurai class in the Kamakura (1185–1392) and Muromachi (1392–1568) periods, a more masculine attitude came to dominate lacquerware, and a slow change became evident in both form and subject matter. For example, the softer lines of earlier periods were modified, and decorated lacquer boxes became slightly, but perceptibly, squarer and bulkier in profile.

During the Momoyama period (1568–1615) a new, dramatic look emerged, with the advent of lacquers coated in pure sprinkled gold against a solid black ground. Simultaneously, the first Western influences appeared in the style of lacquer called *namban nuri* ("Southern Barbarian lacquer"), with its unusual design and imagery.

Finally, during the Edo or Tokugawa period (1615–1868) a newly emergent wealthy and educated middle class brought new, indigenous forms to lacquer. The *inrō*, a portable, tiered medicine container carried as a personal accessory, became the focus of a lacquer movement supplying work for hundreds of new artisans employing a wide variety of techniques.

The following pages outline the evolution of Japanese lacquer from the origins of its use in Buddhist statuary to its emergence as a major art form in its own right—an evolution paralleling that of Japanese culture itself. Lacquer played an important part in Japan's early art history, and the country's love affair with it has lasted over fourteen hundred years.

THE ASUKA AND NARA PERIODS: LACQUER AND BUDDHIST SCULPTURE

During the seventh and eighth centuries the Japanese welcomed foreign influence to an extent that was never repeated until their encounter with the West in the nineteenth century. The historian Langdon Warner wrote, "In all history one finds, perhaps, no people so ripe for a superior culture [referring to China] as the Japanese of that day who had been so long denied it, no people more fit to use it when it came."[6] It is assumed that the Buddhist ritual implements and sculpture of the Asuka and Nara periods, that is, from the middle of the sixth to the end of the eighth century, directly reflected Tang dynasty Chinese models. Lost today are the historical records that would explain why objects in Japanese Buddhist temples during this era were almost all made of lacquer. Presumably Japanese Buddhists were following the Chinese in their forms of religious expression. All that is known, however, is that the Japanese court required an inordinate amount of *urushi*, or lacquer.

This sap, derived from trees thought to have been originally introduced into Japan from China or Korea, was so important to the court that it became a form of tax payment for the upper classes.

After the institution of the Taika Reforms of 645, a special department known as the Office of the Guild of Lacquer Works was created. The adoption of a structured guild system which separated the various aspects of harvesting, refining, and production of a finished product, in this case lacquer, reflected the prolonged influence of the Chinese Tang court, with its strict organization and codification of laws. finally, in 701, with the advent of the Taihō Code, a department of lacquer was established under the Ministry of Finance, consisting of twenty master lacquerers and their various foremen and assistants. All objects made with *urushi* not required for use by the imperial court itself were to be inventoried and granted permission for sale. All households of a certain class required to plant from forty to one hundred trees annually, a fixed amount of lacquer was levied as a tax,[7] and a tithe of one pint of *urushi* a year per young man of a certain station was mandated by law.[8]

After the trees were harvested and the sap was refined, the *urushi* was then delivered to the guild's new location in the city of Nara, which by 710 had become Japan's capital city and the center for the imperial family and the ruling Buddhist factions. All secular and religious business transactions were concentrated there so that strict supervision was possible with the least amount of travel. It has been said that at one time the city of Nara was one massive construction site, a center for the society's cultural production. Certainly Buddhism was the underlying stimulus for all the artistic undertakings of this period, although the Japanese looked upon their products as religious objects rather than as art.

Within the brief span of approximately one hundred years, the lacquer process that grew to dominate Buddhist sculpture evolved through various stages, only to abruptly disappear. The first variation of a dry-lacquer technique called *kanshitsu* was imported from China and appeared in late Asuka sculpture. Lacquer was first mixed with powdered clay and punk, forming a thick, sweet-smelling malleable compound that handled much as dough, and was shaped into the jewelry or hair ornaments used as the accessories for simple wooden images. Since the lacquer workers of the time were brought over from China and Korea,[9] the general appearance of these statues reflected a Chinese aesthetic.

Almost simultaneously, clay religious images were also introduced, presumably from China. The use of clay alone proved not to accord with Japanese sensibilities. Clay did provide, however, the basis for a new and complicated style of sculpture called "hollow dry lacquer" (*dakkan shitsu*). In this method, the statue was first molded of clay. After it had dried, a mold of it was taken, possibly of some form of papier mâché stiffened with rice paste. The clay image was then destroyed, and the remaining hollow mold was lined with hemp soaked in lacquer. An additional mixture of bark and lacquer was pressed against this cloth lining, to reinforce it and provide greater solidity and bulk. A wood armature was sometimes added for support to keep the lacquer from sagging. When the lacquer form had hardened, the outside mold was destroyed. As these images were made in sections, the joins were bonded and smoothed with the addition of a compound made of lacquer stiffened with sawdust or similar material. Lacquer and pigment were further applied to disguise the joins, and the final freestanding life-sized image was given a finishing polish and decorated with colors and gold leaf.[10] Because they were so light, such statues could be easily transported to distant temples.

Unfortunately there were many problems with this hollow-dry-lacquer technique. It was complex, too laborious, and used too much lacquer. In addition, the lacquer image was hidden from view during much of the production process, making it difficult to determine whether the substance had dried completely without slippage. Because of this, a simpler method was developed. This consisted of lacquer-soaked hemp being applied directly to the surface of a clay image, and additional thickening layers subsequently added. But here too, there were many technical difficulties. For example, the wet hemp adhered to the unbaked porous clay, contact that tended to dissolve the surface of the image. Another problem was shrinkage of the cloth during drying. Other obstacles can only be guessed at, as no written records are extant.

At any rate, this and other variations of the technique were suddenly abandoned, undoubtedly because of their expense. The oldest and greatest extant examples of the hollow-dry-lacquer method were products of the great Nara workshops and may still be seen there today. One dates from the year 734 and may be found at the temple Kōfukuji, while an equally superb set of images from circa 742–47 is housed at the Sangatsudō subtemple of the Tōdaiji complex. Unfortunately, as the Nara period came to an end so did the resources of the national treasury. With the exception of the exquisitely sensitive portrait of the famed Buddhist priest Ganjin (687–763), created in 763, hollow-dry-lacquer statues became too expensive to be viable as a vehicle for religious art. That such lacquer statues have survived over twelve hundred years serves as a tribute to the durability of the medium.

In the course of the eighth century, lacquer alone as a medium for religious sculpture was replaced by the more easily controlled hybrid of wood embellished with lacquer, in which the artist could express himself more directly. The wood-lacquer combination was already familiar to native artisans who had begun to replace those imported from abroad. By the time wood had become the prime vehicle for religious sculpture, Japan had developed a guild system with well-trained native sculptors. These gifted artisans, displaying both imagination and skill, drew on all the best features of earlier, previously discarded techniques, but with new maturity and style.

The new wood-core dry lacquer technique called *mokushin kanshitsu*, like that of the previously described sculptures, called for the use of a compound of powdered clay, ground incense, and *urushi,* which was applied in finishing the wood sculpture. Sweet-smelling products were added because they lent the lacquer both mass and a pleasing odor that was supposed to facilitate meditation. Today wood remains the primary medium for religious sculpture and related objects.

THE SECULAR USE OF LACQUER MASKS

By the eighth century, as Japanese artisans began to feel at home in the medium, religious lacquer techniques were adapted to secular purposes. Particularly notable were the large theatrical masks for the imported dance-drama *gigaku* that had been adopted by the Japanese court. These fully formed, colorful sculptures, many of them made of dry lacquer, were created for the aristocracy's amusement. Although quite large, somewhat grotesque in expression, and certainly cumbersome, these extraordinary masks were light enough to be worn by dancers. Despite their exposure to the elements in the course of many outdoor performances, about two hundred examples that have endured may be seen in the Hōryūji Treasures section of the Tokyo National Museum. Other examples are in the national repository known as the Shōsōin, as well as at two great Nara temples, Tōdaiji and Hōryūji.

DECORATIVE TECHNIQUES

The first purely decorative techniques employing lacquer were introduced from China during the seventh and eighth centuries. They were used for religious paraphernalia, such as sutra boxes and portable shrines, as well as for musical instruments. Most early techniques did not survive in their initial form, as the Japanese were not satisfied with the results. These procedures were classified according to whether they were used for the ground or the pictorial element of the composition.

The ground. In the technique known as *heijin* (literally, "flat dust"), irregularly shaped, rather coarse particles of metal were sprinkled sparingly over moist lacquer covering a solid black lacquer undercoat. Particles called *yasuri fun* were created by rubbing a file (*yasuri*) repeatedly over a gold metal bar to create a coarse powder (*fun*). When dry, the grainy lacquered surface was polished down until the sparkle of gold was revealed, and then repolished very carefully until smooth. A simple but expensive technique, it reigned as the underlying background for designs on lacquer for about two hundred years.

Pictorial elements. One of the most enduring materials introduced from China was shell, used either as an inlay or sprinkled on a black lacquer ground that had not yet hardened. For inlays, mother-of-pearl (*raden*) was set flush into a precisely corresponding cutout on the surface of the object, utilizing lacquer as the adhesive. Through the centuries and into modern times, a variety of shells, used in a number of techniques, have played an important role in the creation of surface designs in Japanese lacquer.

Gold and silver powders (*kingin*) were also used for decoration, applied in three ways: *makkinru, kingin-e,* and *maki-e. Makkinru* is the precursor of the *maki-e* procedure known as *togidashi.* It was achieved by sprinkling coarse gold filings over the freshly lacquered, moist lines of a drawing. When the ground had dried, a thin overcoat of lacquer was applied only once and then polished down in the same way as in the *heijin* method, but unfortunately the gold in the textured surface flaked or wore off with use. In *kingin-e,* gold or silver powder was mixed with glue and the picture drawn directly on the ground. But here, too, the exfoliation of the textured surface became a problem

Maki-e, meaning literally "sprinkled picture," was a purely Japanese innovation. In this technique, as in *makkinru*, the design was first drawn on the ground in lacquer, and while it was still wet, metal powders were shaken on the sticky lines or areas. After they had dried, additional thin coats of lacquer were applied to fix the particles to the base. The surface was sometimes lightly polished at this point. This differed greatly from the traditional Chinese method of mixing the metal or color with the lacquer and then applying it directly to the ground, much the way that oil paints are applied to canvas.

In the decorative method called *heidatsu*, thick gold or silver sheets were inlaid into the surface of the object, after which additional coats of lacquer were applied and separately polished. Each polishing revealed the underlying metallic surface. *Heidatsu* was supplanted after about a century by the popular *hyōmon* method, in which the decorative image or pattern was cut from thin sheets of beaten gold or silver, and pasted onto a finished surface.

In the *yūshoku* method, pigments in paste form were brushed onto the design, after which the surface was covered with an oil and left to dry. Again, chipping and exfoliation were problems, and this technique became obsolete.

Out of all the Chinese methods introduced in this early period, only those involving mother-of-pearl inlay remained unchanged. Otherwise, variations that were the result of trial and error were responsible for the development of lacquer as an art. Innovations driven by the determination, passion, and patience of Japanese craftsmen made it possible for the early, simple *maki-e* procedure to evolve into the most complex repertoire of lacquer techniques in the world.

THE HEIAN PERIOD:
LACQUER OBJECTS FOR PERSONAL USE

In order to avoid the political influence of the Buddhist monasteries so firmly entrenched in Nara, the imperial court moved to the city of Heiankyō (now Kyoto) in 794 after a brief move to another location. As the extraordinary amount of lacquer required for use by the religious establishments declined, the source of patronage shifted to the court aristocrats, whose taste was more secular. At about the same time, the Tang dynasty of China, which had contributed so richly to Japanese culture and art, became unstable, and in 838 the Japanese ceased sending official envoys to the continent. Thus, in comparative isolation from direct foreign influence, Japanese lacquer art began to evolve independently, expressing a more indigenous sense of style focused on the native poetic sensibility.

The Office of the Guild of Lacquer Works was dissolved and a new system established in which all elements of the lacquer art, including its processing and artisans, were combined under the authority of the Imperial Bureau of Works. Nevertheless, the imperial house and noble families were also able to patronize their own personal lacquerers, a practice that quickly grew, with the result that the objects produced reflected individual taste. This new type of patronage led to innovations in both form and technique. Suddenly *maki-e* was being used to decorate sword scabbards, saddles, palanquins, and carriages. Buddhist statuary and ritual objects also reflected the increased interest in lacquer, as did the accoutrements of an aristocratic lady's toilette, notably the "hand box," or *tebako*, a container filled with smaller boxes used for cosmetics and other personal items. New lacquer compounds and methods of gold decoration soon evolved.

The *tebako*, earlier introduced from China, now became popular among the women of the court. A Japanese historian has hypothesized that its continental precursor was probably equipped with a fitted inner tray holding three smaller containers: one for cosmetics, the second a box for writing implements, and the third for incense. He reasons that as highborn Japanese women needed more room for small boxes to hold the paraphernalia needed for the increasingly fashionable practice of tooth-blackening (see entry 1), the writing box was removed and the space quickly filled with several smaller containers. He concludes that by the eleventh century, the six most common boxes within the *tebako* were two small rectangular boxes for tooth-blackening materials, a square box for white face powder, a large round box for the circular hand mirror, and two small rounded containers for incense.[11] The inkstone box, which was used to hold writing implements such as an inkstone, water dropper, and brushes, blossomed as a separate and distinct object. Literary-minded patrons had these boxes decorated in gold with poignant poetic allusions.

A slightly different insight into the history of the hand box appeared in 1987, when the Chinese lacquer scholar Wang Shixiang published a book on lacquer-decorated objects found in recent Chinese excavations. Among them was a circular, fitted, double-tiered container that held seven smaller covered boxes in one tier and a rounded mirror in the second. Remarkably, this lacquered cosmetic container dates to the Western Han dynasty (AD 25– 240).[12] A fortunate find for an art historian, this unique and ancient box retains all its original fittings. Similar examples of another type from the same era are equally well preserved. One of these, a single-tiered, rounded cosmetic container, holds a brass mirror, knives, hairpins, seals, combs and five small covered containers.[13] Certainly these newly discovered pieces are early examples of the boxes that evolved in China and eventually found their way to Japan. Without further evidence, however, it is not possible to elaborate on the method and exact era of the transmission of either of the two types.

DECORATIVE TECHNIQUES

During the Heian period the purely Japanese *maki-e* method of sprinkling metal powders matured. This method dominated lacquer decoration as the introduction of new techniques enlarged its scope.

The ground. One of the new techniques was *togidashi*, a more sophisticated form of the burnishing technique previously discussed as *makkinru*, in which the decoration and ground appear on one level, without additional coats of lacquer. *Togidashi* is achieved by burnishing the raised applied design. After the gold powders are applied to form it, additional layers of black lacquer are added in order to completely cover this metallic under-composition. Charcoal and water are next carefully used to rub down the black overcoats until the under-design is revealed, dramatically set off against its surrounding black frame. This technique was used in conjunction with other materials such as mother-of-pearl inlay. As very few Heian boxes are extant and no contemporary descriptions are available, the specific details of these early techniques must be conjectured on the basis of records from the eighteenth century and later.

In the case of *ikakeji*, or "poured-on ground," which was also introduced during this period, slightly coarse gold or silver filings were sprinkled on the surface so heavily that only one application was required to achieve a solid metallic finish. Later on, this technique, using much more finely ground powder, became known as *fundame*.

Pictorial elements. New color effects were achieved by the blending of gold and silver powders (*aokin fun*) in various proportions, a combination that allowed the artist gradations in tone, and therefore the subtle nuances that the aristocracy admired.

Finally, in the Heian period wood supplanted the lacquered hide that had occasionally been used for the forms or core of objects, as well as the the dry-lacquer technique found in ancient Buddhist sutra boxes.

The few extant examples show that the sides and tops of Heian-period lacquered objects had gently curved surfaces. During this period a metal rim was used to reinforce both the top and bottom edges of the box's components, guarding the most exposed and fragile parts of the box from chipping or cracking through use. It also protected the box from warping. A few sources suggest that this edging was made of a pewter-like metal called *byakuro*, and most also agree that it was used only during the Heian period.[14]

THE KAMAKURA PERIOD: THE TASTE OF THE SAMURAI

For more than 350 years, while the imperial court indulged itself in questions of aesthetics, its defense was relegated to the samurai, warrior families that began as offshoots of the aristocracy who established their bases of power in outlying regions. These protectors of the court gradually came to dominate it as they vied with each other for control. There was a great war, which ended in 1185 with a victory establishing the hegemony of the Minamoto family. Minamoto no Yoritomo (1147–99) was declared shogun in 1192, and moved the center of political power (though not the imperial capital) to his base in the northeastern town of Kamakura. The form of military protectorate he pioneered endured for approximately 650 years.

The new samurai patrons of the arts had their own influence on the art of lacquer. By the thirteenth century a change in the general shape of lacquer boxes became evident, as a squarer profile replaced the gentle curves of the Heian period. In *tebako*, for example, a ratio of 1:5 between the height of the lid and the rest of the body was established, which represented an increase over that of the Heian-period *tebako*. Containers for storing scrolls utilized a different arrangement of cords and rings for securing the lid than that of the previous period. A trilobed cutout on either side of the lid was invented that permitted the metal side-ring attachments for the cords on the lower section to move up and down without damage to the overlapping lid. This new system of cords kept the top of the box from shifting, especially when used in travel.

DECORATIVE TECHNIQUES

The ground. The subtle color achieved by blending silver with gold that had been a feature of the previous era now gave way to the predominance of gold. As it became more highly refined, so did the techniques employed in its use. Two new grounds evolved.

The first, called *hirame*, used flattened particles. Similar in shape and equal in size, they were sparingly applied to a moist surface, relacquered with a clear coat, and then polished. The second technique, known as *nashiji* because of its physical resemblance to the skin of a Japanese pear, consisted of irregularly shaped particles of gold sprinkled fairly evenly on a black ground that had been polished and then covered with a coat of translucent lacquer. After the adhesive coating had dried and the particles were firmly glued to this base, several coats of a transparent yellowish-orange lacquer tinted with gamboge were applied and polished in succession. *Nashiji* was so admired that it quickly replaced the simpler *heijin* style.

Pictorial elements. The introduction of two new techniques called *hira maki-e* and *taka maki-e* changed for all time the treatment of depth and dimension in lacquer box designs. *Hira* (low) *maki-e* usually employs only one level of powder above the ground. A layer of gold powder, either in various tones or pure, was sprinkled on the semi-wet lacquer that had been used to draw the design. After drying, a thin protective layer of clear lacquer was applied to fix the particles, then polished to a high sheen.

In *taka* (high) *maki-e*, the "height" is achieved by the repeated application of *hira maki-e*, built up layer upon layer. Although expensive and time-consuming, it was greatly admired by its patrons. Ultimately, however, it proved too expensive, as well as difficult to control and stiff in impression. Looking for other ways to achieve the same effect, the lacquer artists who created boxes for secular use began to use something called *sabi urushi*, a malleable compound of *urushi*, pumice, and water. *Sabi urushi* added height quickly, was inexpensive to make since it required no gold in its composition, and was easy to both shape and control. Similar to the malleable compound formerly used to mold ornaments for early Buddhist wooden statuary, it afforded greater freedom of expression in lacquer.

Sheet gold (*kanagai*) as well as the thinner, more easily cut *kirigane*, both used originally in decorating sculpture and sutra scrolls, came into use for inlays and highlights. Mother-of-pearl inlay also continued as a major design element during this period. The few extant pieces of Kamakura-period lacquer show expressive lyrical qualities, positive in feeling and not overly complex in their motifs.

Around the thirteenth century, a new, practical lacquerware consisting of vessels for eating and drinking was developed by the Buddhist priests of the temple Negoroji in what is now Wakayama Prefecture. These objects were typically made of wood covered first in black and then finished in red lacquer. The forms had such grace and symmetry that they were only occasionally decorated. Before the temple was burned in the wars of the sixteenth century, many monks had carried the secret of making these objects north to the lacquer-producing area known as Wajima.

THE MUROMACHI PERIOD: AN ERA OF CONFLICT

During the fourteenth century, conflict between two branches of the imperial family, along with the rise to power of the Ashikaga warrior family, resulted in the complete destruction of the Kamakura shogunate. The victorious Ashikaga moved the political center back to the Muromachi area of Kyoto, which gave its name to the period. Due to the continuous uncertainty introduced by frequent warfare, a general melancholy pervaded Japan. Lacquer objects were decorated in subdued tones, and compositions tended to be sober and somewhat contemplative in nature. Re-

newed influences from China were introduced by Zen monks returning from study on the continent. A Chinese style became evident in painting and other pictorial arts, and lacquer was no exception.

Although few new lacquer techniques were introduced during this bleak time, there was a change of focus in lacquerwork as emphasis shifted from the shape of a lacquer box to its decoration. Under the patronage of the reigning shogun Ashikaga Yoshimasa, who died in 1490 after ruling from 1449 to 1474, two great schools of lacquerers became prominent.

The first was the Igarashi school, founded by Igarashi Shinsai (active mid-fifteenth century), which was associated with the Higashiyama style (named for the location of Yoshimasa's villa). Its distinctive look depended on increased use of *taka maki-e* techniques combined with *togidashi*. This multilevel effect was termed *shishiai maki-e*.[15] The second, the Kōami school, was started by the great Kōami Michinaga (1410–78) and carried on by his son Kōami Michikiyo (1433–1500). Michikiyo was commissioned to decorate furniture for the enthronement of a late-fifteenth-century emperor. Distinguishing between the work of these two schools is difficult. It has been suggested that early Kōami lacquers used designs by Tosa Mitsunobu (1434–1525), Nōami (1397–1471), and Sōami (?–1525).[16] The Kōami eventually superseded the Igarashii when they were chosen to decorate furniture for Toyotomi Hideyoshi (1537–98), the warrior-ruler of the late sixteenth century. Traditionally this school had been inspired by master painters of the court, especially those of the Kanō school, founded by Kanō Masanobu (1434–1530), whose style was originally based on Chinese paintings.

In lacquer works, silver and gold sheet metal became more widely used to highlight monochromatic color schemes in which only gold and silver powders and their combination (known as *aokin*) were used. Domed shapes were flattened completely—

presumably to accommodate the heavier buildup of lacquer encouraged by the increased use of *sabi urushi*.

Stylistically, literary themes became the almost exclusive subject for the writing-implement box known as the *suzuribako*. During the Muromachi period, poems in the fluid *hiragana* script, executed in the raised letters called *uta-e,* were carefully integrated into the decoration of the exterior of the box and its interior components, with silver added for highlights. Subject matter sometimes reflected scenes from *The Tale of Genji* and allusions to established famous places (*meisho-e*). But, again, due to the times, the mood was one of introspection and melancholy. A favored mode of expression was the use of lightly sprinkled gold against an increasingly dominant black ground, with decoration most often involving landscapes replete with seasonal symbols.

THE MOMOYAMA PERIOD: A TRIAD OF NEW STYLES

Generally speaking, three styles of lacquer prevailed during the brief Momoyama period, when the strongest force in the development of the art was exerted by the soldier-statesman Toyotomi Hideyoshi. Directly or indirectly, he was responsible for the development of two of the three styles that dominated lacquer for nearly a century after his time.

Historians have described Hideyoshi's passion for gold and how he rewarded the services of his followers with lacquers heavily embellished with it. Moreover, his taste for the exotic resulted in an innovative style that reflected in pictorial form the visiting foreigners of the time. That style, one of the three mentioned above, is known as *namban nuri,* or "Southern Barbarian lacquer." (The term *namban,* or Southern Barbarian, applied to all Western visitors to Japan, supposedly refers to the direction from which they arrived). The most exotic pieces of *namban nuri* show figures of visiting Europeans—chiefly

Portuguese and Dutchmen. Designs based on European taste, combined with the prevailing Japanese artistry of the Kyoto area, were responsible for an abundance of exports to Europe. However, because of the suppression of Christianity in the first half of the seventeenth century, few *namban nuri* pieces have survived. Objects decorated only with Western design motifs such as the one shown in this collection (see entry 10) were produced until about 1650.

The second major style to be introduced on lacquer boxes during the Momoyama period was again due to Hideyoshi. The Toyotomi had become patrons of the Kōami family of lacquer artists, and Hideyoshi's taste is best reflected in what became known as the Kōdaiji style of lacquers. Kōdaiji is a temple about a mile east of the Kamo River in Kyoto, built at the behest of Hideyoshi's wife in 1605, seven years after her husband's death. This impressive memorial contains examples of the finest lacquerwork of the period. Assembled in Hideyoshi's mausoleum are outstanding examples of the style to which the temple gives its name, although some of them, such as those used for food service, were brought there from their former home in Hideyoshi's castle at Fushimi.

The temple became known for these pieces, as well as for the ornate mausoleum, in which the wood paneling, doors, and parts of the raised dais are elegantly decorated with imaginative designs created by members of the Kōami family. Shimmering gold of various thicknesses, fashioned in straight lines and curves, is set off by the rich solid black of the undecorated ground. In the dim, filtered light, this gold reflects what little illumination is available. In shadow especially, one can begin to appreciate the artists' original intent, and rich pools of solid black are made even more intense by the darkness of their setting. The Kōdaiji style was elegant and simple (see entries 11–14 for examples of it). Here literary imagery was replaced by configurations using geometric designs and floral images, mainly associated with autumn.

The most characteristic design and innovation of the Momoyama period was the use of *nashiji* in the image itself rather than simply as a ground. This approach is termed *e-nashiji*, or "pictorial *nashiji*" and typified the Kōami lacquers of this period. Another new method introduced on the more elaborate Kōdaiji lacquers was the abundant use of *keuchi*, an outline technique in which thin edges around flowers, leaves, and the like are raised with the addition of gold-sprinkled *taka maki-e*. Two other innovations were *hari-gaki* (literally, "needle drawing") in which a sharp instrument such as a quill is used to scratch away the sprinkled gold so that the plain, black ground appears in the veins of leaves; and *kakiwari*, in which the veins of leaves are left in reserve, also allowing the black background to supply the contrasting color.

The third style that prevailed during the Momoyama era was the Higashiyama style of lacquer, introduced in the Muromachi period and associated with the Igarashi masters. In time however, though still well regarded, growing partiality for the Kōami heralded the end of patronage for the Igarashi school. Eventually the Igarashi family left Kyoto, and went north to the area known as Kanazawa.

The Edo Period:
Maturation of the Lacquer Arts

The middle of the seventeenth century was marked by a flourishing of popular culture similar to that which had begun in Europe some three centuries earlier. This economic and cultural revolution was unintentionally instigated by the new Tokugawa shogunate, which little dreamt of the far-reaching consequences of regulations it had imposed to keep the samurai families under control.

In keeping with the ideas of Neo-Confucianism, which had been adopted as the official state philosophy, the ruling samurai class was taught to view the handling of money with distaste, as something undig-

nified. Hence, the samurai found it necessary to use members of the merchant class as brokers in order to exchange their allotted governmental stipend, in the form of rice, for money. Amounts not needed for food were converted into cash in a special exchange opened just for that purpose, controlled and operated by the merchant class.

A second momentous action that effected dramatic changes within Edo society was the imposition of government regulations that mandated regular travel to attend the shogun at his capital of Edo on the part of the lords (daimyo) of the some 250 domains into which the country was divided. The wives and children of the daimyo were permanent hostages in their Edo residences, while the daimyo themselves alternated between residence in the capital and visits to their home territories in order to collect taxes and otherwise preside over their administration. This travel was required to take place every six months to two years, depending on the distance of the daimyo's fief from Edo. Each provincial lord required an entourage for the journey in keeping with his station. This resulted in the spending of enormous sums of money to feed, clothe, and pay the staff required for the long and arduous trip, and to buy gifts to give the shogun and his family upon return to the capital. The shogunate intended these expenditures to bleed provincial lords of extra funds so they would not be able to finance rebellion against it.

In fact, the practice of alternate attendance, or *sankin kōtai*, resulted in the transfer of such immense sums of money into the hands of the merchants that by the end of the seventeenth century they either directly or indirectly controlled most of the nation's cash. These newly rich patrons of the arts were now able to buy things that only their betters could previously have afforded. Great quantities of gold-decorated lacquer articles were ordered and the small portable medicine carrier known as the *inrō* (see entry 34) became the most prized personal adornment of members of the merchant class—aside from the occasional single sword that a few of them, with special permission, were allowed to wear.[17]

As the passion for lacquered objects increased, many well-established lacquerers from Kyoto were invited to move to the fast-growing city of Edo. Soon new families of artisans sprang into being, introducing innovative shapes and techniques reflecting the adventurous spirit within the shogunal capital. In the old imperial capital of Kyoto, the more established schools remained where they were, or established branches in the Kanazawa and Wajima areas. Old techniques were refined, and unusual combinations of media were more quickly accepted by customers perhaps less cultured, but also less conservative than the aristocracy. Moreover, these merchants quickly developed their own culture and sense of style.

At the same time, the aristocrats still required traditional lacquered objects that comprised the bridal trousseau: cosmetic boxes, incense game sets, boxes for the tea ceremony, and other objects. These lacquers were usually emblazoned with the crests of the two families that were to be united by the marriage. The seventeenth and eighteenth centuries indeed represent both a renaissance and the final phase in the development of the lacquer arts.

Eventually, without stimulation from the outside world, creativity in this closed society diminished. With excessive demand and dwindling imagination, decadence set in, and lacquer decoration grew repetitious and banal.

The Meiji Restoration in 1868 brought with it the introduction of Western dress, making *inrō* obsolete.

Only two or three great lacquer artists of the late nineteenth century created lacquers of distinction, while many spent their time making copies of older pieces. *Kinji*, the sprinkled gold ground that could be polished to a high shine, represented the new age. Flash and dexterity in techniques dominated the field. Speed replaced care, and the new, uneducated foreign patrons of the art did not learn to recognize quality in lacquer for some time. From the late 1880s until the 1970s, with a few exceptions, lacquerware tended to degenerate in quality and technique. In the latter part of the Meiji period, imitations, especially of eighteenth century *inrō*, were exported and became known as "Yokohama" copies, after the port from which they were marketed abroad.

In recent years, especially since the 1980s, new generations of young artists working in mixed media are creating contemporary lacquers in both figurative and abstract formats. Regional lacquerers also preserve their own traditions in the production of gifts and practical items. In the examples shown in this text of the popular *tsugaru nuri* (see entry 25) and *wakasa nuri* (see entry 55) techniques, we see basic provincial styles being used primarily as a backdrop for further decoration.

Today lacquer production has become greatly simplified, with alternate materials often used to achieve the same visual effects seen in earlier pieces. Antique boxes such as those that can be seen in this book are becoming more and more a rarity, to be treasured and cared for. They represent a time, a sense of place, and an aesthetic perception that are rapidly vanishing from a fast-changing culture.

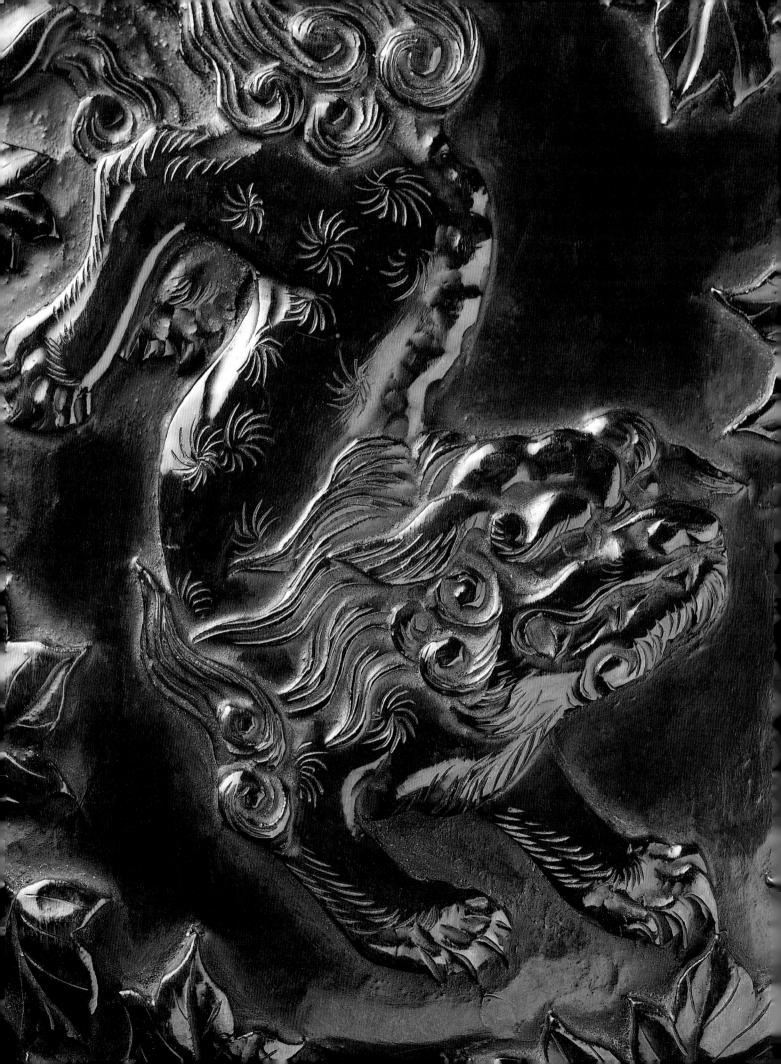

The Collection

1

Rectangular box for tooth-black (ohagurobako)

Design of a flowering plum tree.

Muromachi period, late 15th or early 16th century.
Dimensions: L 2 ¾ in x W 2 ⅛ in x H ⅞ in
(6.9 x 5.4 x 2.2 cm)

Boxes for tooth-black (*ohaguro*) of this general shape and size were originally part of a set of containers for cosmetics and other personal items found inside a larger *tebako*, or "hand box" (see entry 9), an ensemble thought to have been introduced to Japan from China during the early Heian period (794–1185). Over time, many of the components of the matched *tebako* sets were misplaced and most are now incomplete. The boxes for tooth-black were sought after by collectors during the sixteenth century as containers for the incense used in the newly popular tea ceremony. Their size, shape, and elegant finish perfectly suited them for holding the precious scented wood which, when burned, exuded an aroma that calmed the mind.

Beginning in the Heian period it was the custom for aristocratic married women to apply an oxide of iron to the front teeth.[1] Tooth-black is believed to have been introduced to Japan from Polynesia and Southeast Asia.[2] It was prepared by pouring rice wine or vinegar over iron nails or filings, which were then kept in a warm place for several days. Afterward, the excess liquid was poured off and the remaining solution filtered through a cotton cloth until a solid substance had accumulated. This black material was then repeatedly applied to the teeth until the desired color and effect were attained.[3] Tooth-blackening persisted until the fall of the Tokugawa shogunate in the nineteenth century.

The flattened style of the landscape decorating the outer surface of the lid of this box is typical of the Muromachi period, when frontal imagery dominated lacquer designs. The term frontal imagery is used here to denote an early style of composition in which little spatial differentiation is attempted, resulting in a two-dimensional effect. This stylistic device is most frequently found in landscape motifs on lacquers from the fourteenth to seventeenth centuries, and variations on it will be noted in later entries.

Gold particles sprinkled on a jet background suggest snowfall at night. A gentle wind disturbs the surface of the flowing water, creating small waves that lap against the shore. The buds of the flowering tree appear freshly opened. A moment of observation brings to mind one of the countless poems that dwell on the inner strength of the plum and its blossom-laden branches:

> The four seasons are like spring.
> Even in the ninety days of summer I imagine
> I see a bit of snow and the plum's crooked shape.
> In the dark I smell its fragrance
> Carried by the breeze.[4]

During the Muromachi period, the softness of Chinese Yuan-dynasty painting heavily influenced Japanese painting and lacquerwork. Yet at the same time the Kanō school established itself in Japan, with distinctive and characteristic stylistic mannerisms derived from Southern Song academic painting. As a result, a single composition might include a mixture of several painting styles.

Here, the two softly intertwined main branches of the tree and the gently rounded hills demonstrate Yuan influence. Conversely, the angular strokes of the tree trunk (a feature of Kanō painting) along with its sharply jutting branches express the strength of Zen ink-painting styles derived from earlier Chinese models.

Seven large flowers dominate the tree, with countless small buds suggesting life to come. Three blossoms of exaggerated size, composed of mother-of-pearl inlay, add textural contrast. The dull matte gold (*fundame*) of the four equally large remaining flowers gives a more subtle effect. The stamens and pistils of the flowers are precisely drawn in gold *hira maki-e*. The rest of the blossoms and buds are executed in a combination of *hira maki-e* and *taka maki-e* techniques. Small square-cut pieces of silver and gold (*kirigane*) have been added to highlight the contour of the tree trunk.

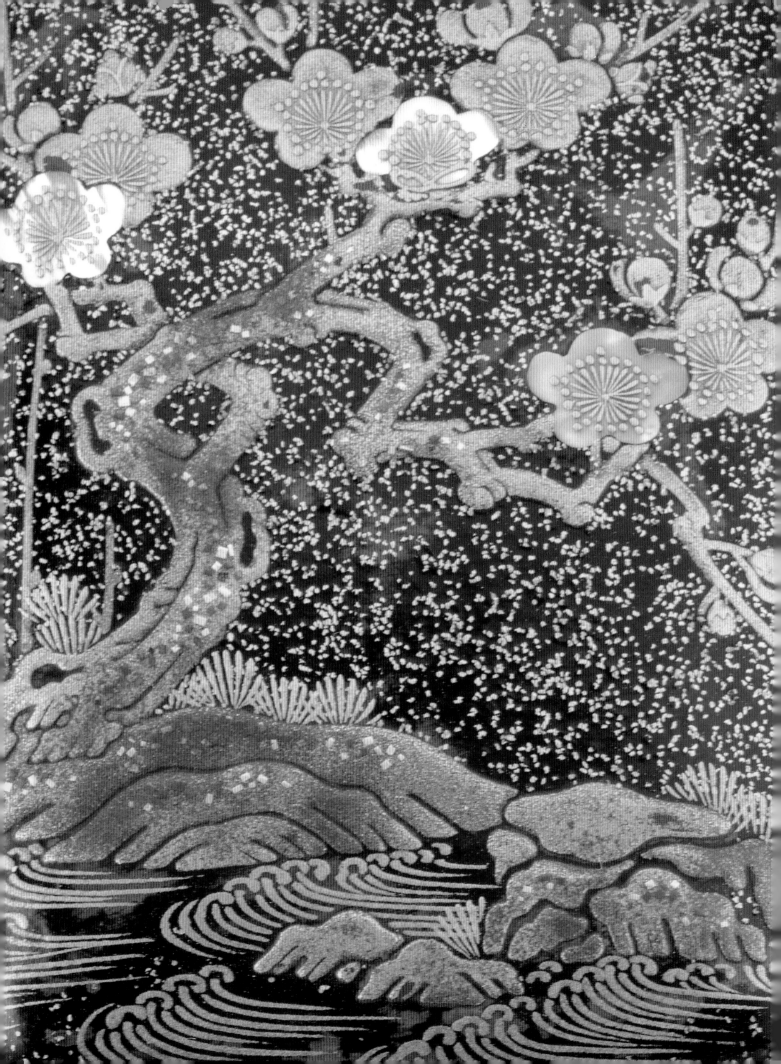

All of this decoration lies atop a lightly sprinkled, flattened-gold-particle ground called *hirameji*. The simple black ground of the inside of the box is similarly decorated.

Dark lead rims protect the outer edges of both the top and bottom of the box.[5] Especially during the Kamakura and Muromachi periods, metal-rimmed boxes such as this fit "mouth to mouth" in what is termed the *aikuchi-zukuri* style.

CONNOISSEURSHIP: At first glance, the general appearance of the ground suggests the use of sprinkled gold particles in a technique known as *nashiji* because of its resemblance to the skin of a Japanese pear. However, a closer look reveals that the particles are nearly uniform in size and shape. Their coarseness and flat, rather than curled shapes, common in fifteenth-century lacquer, suggest the piece dates from before the Edo period.

Restoration is visible in the lighter patchy areas of the background, where certain spaces have been expertly filled in. The mother-of-pearl inlaid petals are also later restorations, and the gold flowers have been reworked. The iconography of the composition is equally mixed. For example, the tree and its branches are a late-fifteenth-century motif, while the curling waves in the foreground have typical seventeenth century features. Yet the shape, size, proportion of lid to bottom, "feel" of the box, and its delicate quality are characteristic of early *kōgō*, or incense containers. In sum, there is little doubt that the box and its basic design are of the Muromachi period.

Detail of the lid.

2

Inkstone box (suzuribako)

Design of a large pine tree accompanied by flowering
plum branches heralding the approach of spring.

Late Muromachi or Momoyama period,
late 16th to early 17th century.
Dimensions: L 9 ¼ in x w 8 ⅝ in x H 1 ⅞ in
(23.5 X 21.9 X 4.8 cm)

The inkstone box is a fitted container for writing materials, usually including an ink stick, the inkstone (*suzuri*), a water dropper (*suiteki*), and brushes. Preparation of ink provides a time for meditation. A few drops of water from the dropper are allowed to trickle into the deep hollow well carved at one end of the fitted stone. A specially shaped ink stick, usually rectangular in form, is moistened by dipping the end into the water. The wet edge is then firmly but gently rubbed against the finely grained surface of the flat part of the stone with slow, meditative strokes. The accumulated fresh black liquid is repeatedly pushed into the well until the color, consistency, and viscosity of the ink tells the maker that it is ready.

On the lid of the box, massive clusters of pine needles contrast strongly with the lacquer ground, which is suggestive of a night sky. Their thick silhouettes seem almost too heavy for the thinner branches from which they grow in fanlike contours. Close examination shows that an extraordinarily skilled, steady hand painted each individual pine needle. The flowers and buds exhibit detailed perfection of form, with the outer edge of every petal delineated in the raised outline technique known as *keuchi*. The use of a black underpainting, in which dimension is suggested through the use of heavy sprinkled gold in both *hira maki-e* and *taka maki-e* techniques, is typical of the Muromachi period.

During this period, mood was expressed in lacquer through a limited range of techniques, customarily using only two metal powders. Silver, gold, or some combination of the two were employed to achieve an almost monochromatic effect. In this piece, this limited tonal range evokes a feeling of bleakness that pervades the half-light of the winter sky, and lends the composition a rather somber quality.

The use of *sabi urushi*, a thick mixture of pulverized pumice, *seisei urushi*, and water, new in Muromachi-period lacquer, enabled the artist to build up an area higher and faster than the older *taka maki-e* technique of applying successive coats of lacquer. The occasional addition of cut gold (*kirigane*) or silver encrustations that penetrate the lacquer rocks provide subtle contrasts in color and texture.

The small stream in the foreground, juxtaposed against the large pine and flowering plum, suggests an early spring thaw, while the two rocks on either side of it imply permanence and echo the solidity of the heavy pine.

The frontal imaging of the trees, though less striking here than in the previous example, is a device that persisted in landscapes until the seventeenth century. The compositional details, concentrated on the left, are counterbalanced by the empty space on the right. This deliberately assymetrical composition is a characteristically Japanese aesthetic convention that invites the mind to wander undisturbed.

Typically, when an inkstone box is open, the lid rests to the right of the bottom section, side by side, with the inside of the lid facing up. The designs on the two halves of the interior are usually viewed as a whole. There is always a fitted section nesting in the bottom of the box, which contains receptacles for the inkstone and the water dropper.

Here, the fitted section contains two separate, removable trays that once held such implements as writing brushes and a knife used to trim the brushes when their tips wore down.

The type and location of the inkstone, inserted into its own cutout, and the color and shape of the water dropper are very important. Although the water dropper is always located above the inkstone, the arrangement of elements within the fitted bottom section often helps date the box. Here, for example, the ensemble of a plain copper water dropper, an inkstone set in a ridged surround, and two trays, one to each side, is typical of the Muromachi period.

Various seasonal motifs, frequently in complementary pairs, often decorated the inner and outer

Above: interiors of the box and lid. Below: detail of the exterior of the lid.

surfaces of lacquer boxes. In this example, the exterior suggests early spring, and the interior, autumn. The designs on both the inside of the bottom section and the interior of the lid present an almost idyllic vision of autumn. *Hira maki-e* and *taka maki-e* on a *nashiji* ground, the essence of this elegant display, are enhanced by a few rows of diamond-shaped pieces of cut gold (*kirigane*). This "underlining" technique that focuses attention on the lower part of the composition echoes an early convention. The rims of the box are in *fundame*.

CONNOISSEURSHIP: This is one of the finest pieces in the collection. The complex and dexterously executed imagery creates a softly poetic atmosphere, while both the workmanship of the lid and that of the interior are masterly. Nothing was stinted in the materials used. The gold powders for the pine needles, for example, are of the best quality, with no addition of silver as an adulterant, and hence appear pure yellow in tone. The black underpainting apparent in certain worn areas on the cover reveal a lacquer artist who was able to draw directly on the surface. Moreover, the flakes used for the ground are not curled, a characteristic that helps date pre-Edo lacquers. Curling reflected more light and therefore gave the impression of the use of more gold than was actually employed.

3
Inkstone box (suzuribako)

A large pine and a flowering cherry tree are shown intertwined, partially hidden by a rocky promontory.

Edo period, early 17th century.
Dimensions: L 9 in x w 8 ¼ in x H 1 ¾ in
(22.9 x 20.9 x 4.5 cm)

The limbs of the two trees intertwined like the arms of lovers in an embrace give this *suzuribako* a poetic, almost sensual quality. Symbols of the four seasons—the pine (winter), cherry blossoms (spring), flowing water (summer), and the chrysanthemums (fall)—complete the composition, which is executed in two different styles. The angular outlines of the massive rocks, which keep the compositional center of gravity to the left, are a stylistic hallmark of Kanō school painting, already widespread by this time. The stylized wave pattern of the stream in the foreground may be an example of the early-Kamakura-period *tsukegaki* technique, which fashioned fine raised lines by applying thick lacquer to an already finished surface and then dusting with gold powder while the lacquer was still damp.

The wave patterning shown here may be also accomplished in another way. This method begins with an undercoating of black lacquer, finely polished down. An even but thin layer of gold powder is then added and left to dry. This forms an intermediate ground for the rendering of the waves. Then the textured, curved patterning representing the waves is applied in a *taka maki-e* technique similar to the *tsukegaki* technique described above, but employing a thickening agent. First, a layer of lacquer thickened with egg white, or a specially prepared type of lacquer sometimes used for undercoating is applied. When this is about half dry (tacky but fairly firm), a tiny pronged tool resembling a miniature wooden comb, either with or without one slightly dominant tooth, is applied to the surface repeatedly in the desired patterning (see detail, page 44). The teeth pull the overcoating away from the ground with the pressure of each stroke. Fine gold powder is then sprinkled on top of the raised lines. The spume of the water is produced by moving the tool first forward, then back, a technique that results in "puddling,"[6] in this case a desired effect. After the surface is polished, another coat of clear lacquer is applied and it is polished again.

Other areas may be worked at the same time, using other tools to achieve a variety of graphic effects.

The rocks are made out of thick *sabi urushi* covered with gold and embellished with particles of *kirigane* as highlights. A *nashiji* ground represents the sky. Silver is added to certain areas of the chrysanthemums and other flowering plants and grasses that surround the foreground water and rocks, in order to darken them and supply tonal variation.

The ground of the entire composition is of *nashiji*. The edges of the shoreline seem to have been graded down before the surface design was applied, perhaps by shaving the wood of the lid so that the incline was carved into the understructure. In this way the stream below appears to be commanded by a high shore. Careful study of the shape of the box from foreground to background reveals that the artist completed the effect by first adding *sabi urushi* and then applying *taka maki-e* covered with *fundame*.

A few chrysanthemums are rendered as small, well-oxidized silver inlays. Bell flowers and other blossoms and grasses on the shore are executed in *taka maki-e* and *hira maki-e*. Once again the only color contrast occurs where the black undercoating of the gold has come through on the promontory due to wear, an effect also evident in the central parts of various flowers and clumps of pine needle. The *kirigane* that had been added to the large rocks has mostly fallen off.

The inside bottom of the box is divided in half to accommodate a tray on the right for brushes and the inkstone on the left. The colorful silver and cloisonné water dropper differs aesthetically from the rest of the box and is a later replacement, dating from the late nineteenth century. Such replacements are fairly common because of loss or damage to original fittings.

The underside of the lid, placed on the right, shows a full moon of oxidized silver-colored lacquer rising over pampas grasses covered with dewdrops. The light *nashiji* ground suggests dusk. Traditionally, such a scene represents the Musashi plain near Edo,

Above: lid of the box. Below: interiors of the box and lid.

and evokes an atmosphere of solitude and melancholy thoughts of warriors who fell there in ancient battles.

The inside rims of lid, box, and tray are in *fundame*.

CONNOISSEURSHIP: When examining inkstone boxes, attention should be paid to the size, shape, and color of the water dropper, as well as the size of the inkstone and its proportion to the tray. Here, close examination of the cutout for the water dropper shows that it was altered to fit a later replacement. One can see the darkened, irregular outlines of the original cutout, obviously of a different shape.

Detail of the lid.

4
Poem-slip box (shikishibako)

Two pine trees stand against a night sky.

Edo period, late 17th or early 18th century.
Dimensions: L 9 ¾ in x w 8 in x H 2 ½ in
(24.8 x 20.3 x 6.3 cm)

Slips of paper used either for poetic inscriptions or for paintings are known as *shikishi*. Their thickness may vary, but typically the paper is mounted on a kind of cardboard in order to maintain its shape, as application of ink or water-based pigments would cause the paper to wrinkle. The two sizes customarily used are 19.4 cm x 17.0 cm and the slightly smaller 18.2 cm x 16.0 cm.[7] Boxes for the storage of these slips have deep, overlapping lids with cutouts on either side of the bottom edge for ease in lifting the lid. The bottom section usually has small metal rings on each side through which two woven silk cords are attached, their ends joining in a bow at the center to secure the lid.

On the lid of this box, two pine trees, one large and one small, stand as if in defiance of time and the forces of nature. In Japan, famous locales (*meisho*) often function as symbols or metaphors in literature and art. Here, the pines allude to an old legend concerning the twin pines of Takasago and Sumiyoshi. The Noh play *Takasago* by the famed playwright Zeami (1363-1443) describes how the male spirit of the Sumiyoshi pine crosses the sea to Takasago to visit his wife every night. The difference in the sizes of the trees helps them to function as visual metaphors for a man and woman.[8]

The two trees have been lacquered in the difficult *togidashi* technique with some *hira maki-e* to provide contrast on the trunks. The checkered border that surrounds the composition frames the design as if it were a poem slip. The type of alternate patterning used in the border is sometimes called *ishi-datami* (paving stones) because of its resemblance to the paving stones found in Chinese palaces. It is also called *ichimatsu* after an Edo-period Kabuki actor who wore garments with this design on them.

The inside of the lid shows a hanging lantern suspended against the same stark black ground (the type called *ro-iro*) as on its exterior. The interior or lighted area of the lantern is highlighted by minute squares of sheet gold (*kirigane*) that echo the checkered border on the outside of the lid.

CONNOISSEURSHIP: The stunning simplicity of this design is deceptive. Application of the *ro-iro* ground was time-consuming and costly, the finest gold powders were used, and the difficult and delicate *togidashi* technique required an accomplished lacquer artist for its mastery. Of all the techniques available, it requires the most careful hand and eye. Too much polishing (with charcoal) tends to excise the image.

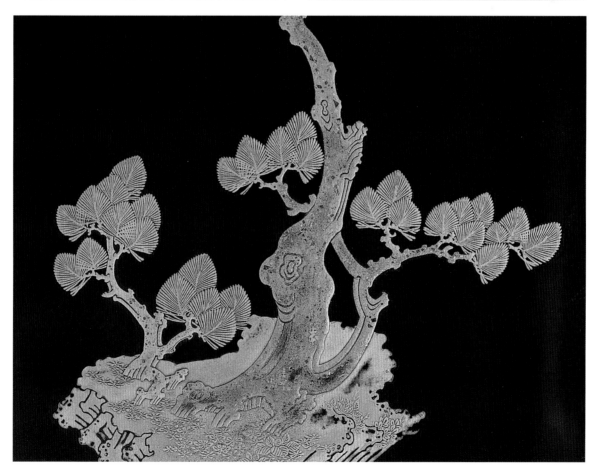

Above left: overview of the box. Above right: interior of the lid. Below: detail of the exterior of the lid.

5
Small box (kobako)

A pine and a plum tree stand on a small hill at dusk.

Edo period, 18th century.
Dimensions: DIA 3 3/16 in x H 1 7/8 in
(8.1 x 4.8 cm)

Small boxes of various shapes, including the circular one shown here, were typically used as incense or cosmetics containers.

The pine tree symbolizes winter, while early spring is suggested in the form of plum blossoms. Set against a ground of black and lightly sprinkled gold, their forms, created in muted tones, project an atmosphere of tranquillity. They seem to emerge from a central point on a hill and flow toward the foreground. Here again, the composition is in what may be termed the "frontal image" format. As in entries 2 and 3, the pine subtly dominates the composition: the accompanying plum tree is almost equal in size but subordinate, originating from behind the trunk of its companion.

The design on this box is an interesting blend of painting styles and lacquer techniques typical of the Edo period. The gently rounded hills show vestiges of the Yuan style, but the firm, strong strokes that define the trees reflect the dominance of the Kanō school. The frontal approach of the composition represents a revival of a style that originated more than three hundred years before. The addition of silver powders defining the interior parts of the plum blossoms is also a very early technique, but the *e-nashiji* ("picture pear-ground") evident here in the trunk of the trees is a late-sixteenth- or early-seventeenth century method. The insides of both lid and bottom are finished in *nashiji*.

The edges of the box have been reinforced in copper, which has been chemically treated to produce a patina known as "fox red."

CONNOISSEURSHIP: Despite the presence of early styles in this box, several features date this to the eighteenth century: its design does not overflow onto the sides, and its rims are not made of lead, but of copper, which was not used to edge lacquer boxes until the eighteenth century. Moreover, the use of silver as a filler and adulterant in the pine needles to lessen the amount of gold needed becomes typical during the Edo period, when lacquer artists sought to cut production expenses while at the same time providing tonal contrast. Finally, the curled edges of the metal flakes signify an Edo-period production.

6
Mirror box (kagamibako)

A pine tree and stalks of bamboo shield a mantled turtle (*minogame*). A crane flies overhead.

Edo period, late 17th or early 18th century.
Dimensions: DIA 5 ⅞ in x H 2 1/16 in
(14.9 x 5.2 cm)

B oxes such as this were used to store the metal mirrors of premodern Japan. Their size distinguishes them from the smaller incense containers known as *kōgō*. Round, hand-held metal mirrors and the techniques for casting them were introduced to Japan from China around the seventh century. The entire mirror was cast as a single piece. Its reflective front surface was highly polished, and the back usually included decoration that encircled a raised central knob pierced by an opening. Typically, a bright, double silk cord with tasseled ends would be passed through it and knotted. The resulting handle allowed one hand to grasp the mirror firmly while the other addressed the hair.

According to Chinese Taoist beliefs, which entered Japan quite early in its history, the universe is divided into two categories: the celestial, represented by the crane, and the terrestrial, symbolized by the tortoise or turtle, both of which also represent longevity in Japanese folklore. Frequently, if a turtle lives a long life, a type of algae or mossy growth attaches itself to the edges of its carapace, from which strands resembling green hair grow, hence the name *minogame*, or mantled turtle.

The design on this box is gracefully executed in the Yuan style with none of the strong sharp lines of the Kanō school of painting, an approach in keeping with the Taoist subject matter. The swirling composition starts at the base of the box and follows, in a free flow, its circular shape. The tree is rooted at the base of the box, stretches up, and spreads its expansive arms, which are clothed in clusters of needles and interspersed with stalks of bamboo. Again, the large central motif is an example of the compositional style described above as frontal imagery. The pine needles (slimmer than those in earlier examples) are executed in gold *taka maki-e*, as are the feathers of the crane and the body of the turtle. The small amphibian is overpowered by the central subject—the pine. The crane seems amused by it all. Only pure gold powders have been used, in a *fundame* technique. The veining of the bamboo leaves is produced by the *harigaki* method, in which the gold powder is scratched away with a quill, a sharpened piece of bamboo, or a needle to reveal the black background.

The interior of the box is of a solid black lacquer that has caramelized to a brownish tone. This is an indication of age, as the iron filings used to make black lacquer have oxidized over time.

CONNOISSEURSHIP: Animals symbolizing longevity were not used to decorate lacquer boxes until the late seventeenth to early eighteenth century. This piece has a free and spontaneous quality, yet the design forms an integrated image covering the entire surface of the box.

7
Document box (ryōshibako)

This large box is decorated with symbols
representing longevity.

Edo period, 18th century.
Dimensions: L 12 ¾ in x W 10 ¼ in x H 8 ½ in
(32.4 x 26.0 x 21.6 cm)

L arge containers for the storage of documents, typically fitted with inner trays, are called *ryōshibako*. The painting style in this example is similar to that of entry 5, except that the structure of the trees and bamboo here reflects the influence not only of the Kanō school, but also that of the celebrated painter Maruyama Ōkyo (1733–95), founder of the Maruyama school.

Ōkyo, although a pupil of the Kanō master Ishida Yutei (1721-86), also studied Western techniques of perspective. That, along with his interest in the art of the Chinese Ming and Qing dynasties, led to his emphasis on the direct observation of nature. As this trend toward realism began to filter into other art forms of the time, eighteenth-century lacquerers also increasingly used these techniques in the service of depicting nature.

On the lid of this box, the ground of the entire composition was first laid down in black lacquer. To define the sky, the artist added *nashiji* as a secondary ground. This two-stage method allowed him to achieve a subtle gradation of tone. Against this background are two separate groves of pine trees interspersed with bamboo. A large stream divides the landscape into two sections, where playful *minogame*, or mantled turtles (see entry 6), scamper on the shores near the water. Three red-crested cranes fly toward their mates, who wait patiently for them on land. Rocks and rolling hills also enliven the scene.

Much time, effort, and expense were required to create this single surface. On the *nashiji* ground the airborne red-crested cranes are made of gold and combined gold and silver particles of varying sizes. Each carefully delineated individual feather helps to enhance the definition of body and wings. A touch of vermilion has been added to the cranes' heads. Nothing has been left to the imagination.

The highly stylized roots of the trees make them seem to stand on their toes, as if dancing. There is movement in the tree trunks, and the clump of needles that fan out from each section are more in proportion to the branches than in any of the previous examples. The depiction of the *minogame* as long-eared, clawfooted griffins rather than as gentle, turtlelike creatures adds a touch of ferocity to an otherwise serene landscape.

The flowing stream has been rendered in the same manner as in entry 3, but the muddy area between the shore and water relies on an experimental method in which the artist used an undercoating of *seisei urushi* (which is naturally dark brown) as a decorative embellishment. This surface has been carefully polished and left in its natural state to add both color and texture to the composition.

The bamboo has been executed in the same meticulous detail as the rest of the greenery. The only difference in method is in the veining of the leaves, which have been scratched away to show the black undercoating. Each leaf is edged in the thin, raised *hira maki-e* style known as *keuchi*. Overall, the composition on the lid appears softer and more flowing than that of previous entries, exhibiting a freedom of execution and an attention to proportion common in eighteenth-century works.

The side panels both repeat and vary the theme of the lid. The inner tray, which rests on the lip of the bottom section of the box, shows a small islet with pines.

Document boxes such as this always had a heavy cord for securing the fairly shallow lid. The metal fittings (*kanamono*) on either side of the box are in dark *shakudō* (an alloy of copper and gold that has been treated to form a black or purple surface). The two metal cord rings are attached to round disks decorated with a bronzed paulownia design.

CONNOISSEURSHIP: A perfect example of an eighteenth-century lacquer box, combining art and practicality. Few of this size and age have survived in a condition as good as that shown here.

Above: overview of the box. Below: exterior of the lid and a detail of its central portion.

8
Tea utensil storage box (chabako)

Fitted with an interior tray. The lid is decorated with
a landscape of a pine tree and other vegetation.

Edo period, 18th century.
Dimensions: L 6 ¼ in x w 3 ⅞ in x H 4 ⅜ in
(15.9 x 9.9 x 11.1 cm)

The tea ceremony (*chanoyu;* literally, "hot water
for tea") came to Japan from China, probably
during the twelfth century. Tea itself had
been introduced in the eighth century, but it was not
until the twelfth century—about the same time the tea
ceremony was introduced by Buddhist monks—that
the seeds for the tea plant were brought to Japan for
cultivation. Because it promotes wakefulness, Zen
monks favored tea as an aid to introspection and meditation. As a formal ceremony grew up around the
drinking of tea, the upper-class military and the aristocracy embraced its use wholeheartedly. Sen no
Rikyū (1521–91), the most influential master in the history of the the ceremony, codified its rules while sim-
plifying its utensils and setting. Since his time the
essential character of the tea ceremony has remained
unchanged, despite variations in such elements as the
time of day for the ceremony, its duration, and the
type of tea consumed.

The tea ceremony has been described as "an art
concealing art, an extravagance masked in the garb of
noble poverty."9 Two basic aesthetic values are associated with this art: *wabi,* the beauty inherent in the
muted and somber, such as the colors rust, burnt
orange, and sienna; and *sabi,* which refers to an aura of
loneliness, as in the sound of an animal calling for its
mate in the quiet of evening, or the sound of evening
rain falling on leaves in an otherwise silent forest.

By the eighteenth century, tea-utensil storage
boxes (*chabako*) such as this one were used to hold
accoutrements such as a teabowl, whisk, and napkin
for a modified tea ceremony while traveling. Like the
present example, the container might also contain a
tray that rested on the inner lip of the ledge in the bottom section and upon which the utensils would be
placed when the set was in use.

The design of this box is simple. A jagged pine
tree with short needles, executed in an abbreviated
style derived from the Zen-influenced ink painting of
the fourteenth century, is silhouetted against a plain
nashiji ground, which also covers all the sides of the lid
and bottom. Matte gold is used both in the foreground and on the borders of the cornering where the
sides of the cover are joined.

When the box is opened, the inside of the lid
reveals a lovely peony blossom on a branch, executed
in *hira maki-e* and *taka maki-e,* with each petal carefully
delineated. The tray is covered in a ground of orange
sprinkled-gold powders against which two birds are
perched in close proximity on a ragged tree trunk.

CONNOISSEURSHIP: Boxes such as this have been poorly
studied, probably because they were essentially travel sets
and did not have the cachet of the tea utensils they held.
It is interesting to compare this piece to the portable
lunch box set of entry 23.

Above: overview of the box. Below: interior of the lid and the fitted interior tray.

9
Hand box (tebako)

A drawered cosmetic container decorated with
motifs representing the four seasons.

Edo period, late 17th or early 18th century. Interior
fitted boxes, 18th century.
Dimensions: L 10 ⅝ in x W 7 ⅜ in x H 5 ½ in
(27 x 18.7 x 14 cm)

Since Heian times, it was the custom for brides
of the aristocracy to bring as part of the wedding trousseau one large lacquered container for
most of their cosmetic needs. This was called a *tebako*,
or hand box. Family crests were usually integrated into
their design motifs. These elaborate boxes were rarely
used, however, and more utilitarian containers graced
ladies' boudoirs. By the late seventeenth century, the
wives of wealthy merchants began to copy this tradition and would own boxes similar to the one shown
here.

The lid. A full moon of silver peeking out of a light
layer of flaked-gold clouds embellishes a perfect
autumn evening. A trio of butterflies hovers over
chrysanthemums in full bloom, pampas grasses, bush
clover, and other autumn flowers and grasses. A wandering stream cuts through small rocks and hills.
Every image is clearly defined in gold *hira maki-e, taka
maki-e,* and an extra layer of gold powder applied for
the veining and the edging of the leaves in the technique called *keuchi.*

Front panel, including drawer. There is a tremendous
feeling of spontaneity in this portrayal of early spring.
A flowering plum tree juts up from behind a brushwood fence. The delicate sprinkling of dull silver
powders on a section of the tree trunk and on a few
blossoms provides shadow and contrast. The petals of
each blossom and bud are outlined further in *hira maki-e,*
as are certain parts of the tree. The brushwood fence
is in the finest of gold *taka maki-e.* The drawer probably stored a mirror, now missing.

Left Panel. Here many symbols represent early to
midsummer. On the right are a blooming peony and
sprouting ferns, partially obscured by a small hill. In
the foreground, the artist has carved into the wood of
the panel and then refinished the resulting lower level
as a running stream. Over a coat of black lacquer, he
has sprinkled gold powders as a base for additional
symbols of water, applied in *hira maki-e.* To emphasize
the current, a degree of "scratching away" (*harigaki*),

executed with the point of a quill, reveals the black
undercoating. This contrasts with the gold to enhance
the intimation of the rocks and pebbles present in the
rushing stream.

A thin layer of fine silver powder has been added
to the underlying black of the peony and its accompanying bud for contrast and depth. This large floral
image throws the balance of the panel's composition
to the right, as it should, for the scene is to be read from
right to left. The mounds of rocks, in *taka maki-e,* are
highlighted near their peaks with the application of
tiny pieces of cut gold (*kirigane*). The stream runs from
right to left, coursing through the small hills and
down a modest incline, rushing by a few rocks, slow-
ing as it passes alongside a patch of irises, and then
flowing on, out of the sight of the viewer. Fireflies
flicker above full-blooming blue irises. Both the
insects and the flowers are minutely detailed in dull
gold (*fundame*), with particles of silver powder added
for subtle contrast. The workmanship is extraordinarily delicate and extremely precise.

Back panel. Wisteria is typically a symbol of early
summer, blossoming from May to June. Noted for its
graceful appearance, this ornamental woody vine is
grown for its decorative value and beloved by the
Japanese. Here the vine is treated with some artistic
license as a jagged, high-rooted tree, perched on a
small rise. On a background of gold *nashiji,* the arched
branches are outlined against seemingly endless space.
Gold florets in long racemes reflect the stillness of
heat. Oxidized silver and tiny cut-gold squares (*kirigane*) give the trunk texture.

Right panel. The pine, representing both winter and
the endurance of life, dominates this side of the box.
A pair of mandarin ducks (symbols of conjugal felici-
ty because they mate for life) are shown swimming,
while two geese on the shore wait for their companion
to alight. The thin gold lines that compose the rounded swirl pattern of the moving water are in a different
style and technique than on the other sides.

Above: overview of the box. Below: exterior of the lid.

Above: front panel. Below: left panel.

Above: back panel. Below: right panel.

Above: components of the set nested in the large box. Below: the complete ensemble.

The Japanese have always considered water an important compositional element, and the way it is depicted usually reflects the season. Here, leaving the background black around the islet on which the pine tree stands heightens the contrast between the swimming ducks and the thin curved lines in gold *hira maki-e* that represent water in movement. At first glance the shoreline looks quiet, but on a closer examination one notices that the arching waves (in gold *taka maki-e*) hit the land with a degree of force. Thus the Japanese viewer would be subtly reminded of the cold associated with the choppy waves of late fall and winter.

Interior fittings. The exterior surfaces of all the smaller boxes that fit so carefully inside this container are covered with an orange-toned *nashiji* ground elegantly decorated with a profusion of passion flowers amid scrolling vines in thick gold *fundame*. Their interiors are finished in vermilion lacquer, and the underside of each piece is sparsely decorated with *nashiji*. The following boxes comprise the interior fittings of this *tebako*.

Box for cosmetic implements. This two-tiered box with a flat lid was used to store such items as brushes for cleaning combs and a spatula to mix the color needed for painting the eyebrows. Dimensions: L 3 ⅝ in x W 1 ¾ in x H 2 ⅜ in (9.2 x 4.4 x 6 cm).

Comb container. An open container for the storage of combs. Dimensions: L 3 ⅝ in x W 3 in x H 2 ⅜ in (9.2 x 7.6 x 6 cm).

Box for face powder. A lidded two-tiered box, with the lower tier used for storing face powder and the upper tier containing a fitted section for the brush used to apply it. Dimensions: L 4 ¹³/₁₆ in x W 3 ¹³/₁₆ in x H 2 ⅜ in (12.2 x 9.7 x 6 cm).

Kamisoribako. A long, rectangular, covered, two-tiered storage box for razors. The top tier is divided to hold three of them. Dimensions: L 7 ⅝ in x W 1 ¾ in x H 2 ⅜ in (19.4 x 4.4 x 6 cm).

Hiire. A container for the ash that is used as a base for the burning of incense. This cylindrical receptacle has a fitted lid with a small knob in the center and its interior is lined in copper. Dimensions: DIA 2 in x H 2 in (5.1 x 5.1 cm).

Jūkōgō. A cylindrical three-tiered covered box. The interior of the bottom section is lined in copper, to be used like the *hiire* described above. The upper two tiers are used to store incense. Dimensions: DIA 2 in x H 2 ¹/₁₆ in (5.1 x 5.2 cm).

Box with domed lid. This cylindrical box resembles a two-tiered box, but there is only a shallow fitted tray within this otherwise hollow container. It probably held either powder, which would be put on the tray for mixing, or hair oil. Dimensions: DIA 2 in x H 2¾ in (5.1 x 6.9 cm).

CONNOISSEURSHIP: There do not seem to be direct design or thematic relationships between this hand box and the fitted boxes within. However, they share a plain gold edging left in reserve between the joining of the panels. This set is probably a "marriage," that is, the making to order of different components of a box when they have been lost or destroyed. Another example of this may be observed in entry 49.

There is an extensive variety in boxes of this type. Some hold items solely for dressing the hair, such as the *kushidai* (literally, "comb stand") and the *tabikushibako*, which was used as a traveling comb box. Because the internal components of boxes such as these had to answer to the requirements of their owner, there was much individual variation.

The workmanship on the case of this *tebako* is of superb quality. The artist shows a unique handling of dimension, as evidenced on the trunks of the pine, wisteria, and plum. He fearlessly applies the high color of pure gold on top of a darker background without any attempt at shading or gradation.

10

A small lacquer chest (dōgubako) in the form of a coffer

The hinged, domed lid and front panel are decorated with leaves, chrysanthemums, and cherry blossoms.

Momoyama period, late 16th or early 17th century.
Dimensions: L 9 ½ in x W 5 ½ in x H 8 in
(24.1 x 13.9 x 20.3 cm)

This is an example of the type of lacquer called *namban nuri*, which consisted of articles made in the European style, or reflecting European themes, during the period of Japan's first contacts with the West in the late sixteenth and early seventeenth centuries. Created strictly for the European market, the objects produced included not only small chests like this coffer, but also desks, tables, secretaries, and chests of other sizes. The designs and techniques that were executed by Kyoto artisans represent a fusion of Chinese, Korean, Japanese, and European taste in items that also include Christian religious symbols.

Christianity was introduced into Japan in the 1540s with the arrival of the Portuguese. In 1549 the charismatic Jesuit priest Francis Xavier arrived in Kyushu, the southernmost main island of Japan. Other missionaries, such as the Spanish Franciscans and the Dutch reformers, followed. Many of the early Westerners were as interested in commercial opportunities as in religious influence, and almost immediately bickering broke out over their efforts to gain the upper hand in one or another of these two spheres. By the beginning of the seventeenth century, rumors of rebellion in the south trickled back to the shogunal capital in Edo, and stringent anti-Christian edicts, targeted at curtailing any insurrection, were issued.

Finally, in the 1630s, recognizing that the previous edicts against the foreign religious zealots had failed, the Tokugawa government acted swiftly and mercilessly. Japanese converts were persecuted, and eventually all Portuguese and Spanish Catholics were permanently expelled from the country. Committed to a policy of isolation, in 1641 the Tokugawa government decided that henceforth only the employees of the Dutch East India Company and a few Chinese nationals would be allowed to trade in Japan, and that this trade would be restricted to the port of Nagasaki. The Dutch trading station was moved from Hirado to Deshima, a tiny island in Nagasaki harbor, to allow tighter surveillance of the foreigners and their activities. Thus began a period of official seclusion that lasted until shortly before the downfall of the Tokugawa regime in 1868.

The *namban nuri* export wares were associated with Christianity, specifically with Catholicism, and during the period of persecution most of the ateliers producing these items were closed. Hence the origin and decline of *namban nuri* are easy to date. These wares are typically decorated with gold, slivers of a tinlike metal and mother-of-pearl inlay set in a mosaic pattern against a black lacquer ground, which through time has turned to dark brown. Although many of the objects were large storage chests, smaller models such as the example shown here were often created for the Spanish market. Extremely portable because of its small size, this type of hinged box may have been used as a pocketbook or a casket for jewelry.

The flowering vines on the chest are rendered in gold lacquer and inlaid mother-of-pearl on the usual black lacquer ground and panels of foliage are separated by bands of a geometric design inlaid in mother-of-pearl. The edging on both the front and back panels of the box follows a mosaic pattern while the quatrefoil design of the edging on the lid and base resembles two crosses. The black lacquer interior is worn and peeling.

Gilded chased brass mountings on the front latch are in the shape of two bulls and are probably original to the piece. The back hinges, decorated with a chrysanthemum design, are later replacements.

CONNOISSEURSHIP: *Namban nuri* was neither produced nor copied after the early decades of the Edo period, and even after the Meiji Restoration of 1868, *namban nuri* reproductions were usually limited to Portuguese or Dutch figures on the portable medicine containers called *inrō*. This allows us to date *namban nuri* boxes with a high degree of certainty to the period prior to Japan's period of isolation from the West.

11

Incense container (kōgō)

Design of sea shells and chrysanthemums.

Momoyama period, late 16th or early 17th century.
Dimensions: DIA 3 ⅜ in x H 1 ½ in
(8.6 x 3.8 cm)

This incense container is in the Kōdaiji style. Kōdaiji *maki-e* is the term applied to a group of lacquers that originated in Kyoto around the beginning of the Momoyama period and continued to be produced into the first half of the seventeenth century. They are designed in a distinctive style, decorated with particular themes, and incorporate unique techniques.

Thematically, most but not all boxes of this category are decorated with a selection from the "seven flowers and grasses of autumn" (*aki no nanakusa*), often in combination with chrysanthemums and perhaps a variation on the paulownia crest of the Toyotomi family. On occasion, as in the example shown here, the design may be divided into two fields by a lightning-bolt geometric motif (*katami-gawari*) originally introduced in the Muromachi period,

Dramatic in appearance, these lacquers have a black ground on which design motifs are usually rendered or outlined with *hira maki-e* in gold, but not necessarily given the typical final sealing coat of lacquer. This technique of omitting the final coat is known as *makihanashi* (literally, "left as sprinkled"). Other decorative procedures virtually exclusive to this Momoyama-period style include the use of *e-nashiji* (literally, "pictorial pear-skin ground"). This technique used throughout a design creates an amber glow which lends an aura to the work. *Harigaki,* in which the black ground is revealed by scratching the gold away with a sharp object such as a needle or quill, is also typical of Kōdaiji *maki-e.*

Due to great demand, most Kōdaiji-style lacquers were produced by ateliers in Kyoto in what approached a production-line atmosphere. However, the workshops of the Kōami family of master lacquerers, who dominated the production of Kōdaiji-style lacquer, held to a high standard.

The Kōdaiji style takes its name from the Zen Buddhist temple Kōdaiji in Kyoto, founded in 1605 by the widow of Toyotomi Hideyoshi as a memorial to her husband.[10] Hideyoshi's mausoleum, known as the Otamaya, is located within the precincts of the temple and contains a number of architectural pieces that exemplify the techniques employed in this style of lacquerwork. First the black ground was applied and allowed to dry. Then additional decoration and the outlines of the design were indicated in red, particularly where gold powders were to be applied. Pieces were completed with only a light final coat of lacquer, if any, leaving the bold designs, composed originally of pure sprinkled gold, without a finishing seal. This proved to be a serious mistake, as it left the unprotected surfaces at the mercy of the elements, which began to do their damage rather quickly after the initial installation of the pieces in the mausoleum. The Otamaya is now undergoing restoration, and a few of the panels used as doors to cabinets within it are now on display in a separate exhibition space constructed for that purpose. Fading on these pieces is so bad that some of the original intent is completely lost.[11]

The incense container shown here is in the Kōdaiji style, but it was probably produced by an individual artist rather than an atelier. No red underdrawing is visible, and the clear lacquer overcoating indicates that it was not mass produced.

The lightning-bolt motif has been used here to bisect the surface of the lid along a diagonal. In the upper half, earth and daylight are suggested by blossoming flowers on a sparkling reflective ground. Below, the sea is represented by a matte-gold darkened ground, in which shells and underwater grasses seem to move with the water's flow. Sunlight in the upper section is intimated by a colorful textured ground employing the *nashiji* technique. The floral foreground, imposed in matte gold (*fundame*) has worn away to reveal the black underpainting.

It is apparent that the artist used a freer, more painterly style in rendering the underwater scene than he did in the other half of the lid. The contrast is probably deliberate. The gentle curved and sloping

Interior of the lid.

contours of the clams are depicted in gold and black *taka maki-e*, thicker than the flowers in the opposite scene, yet just as subtly rendered. Scattered patches of softly-shaded silver powder have been applied to some areas of a conch shell not visible in this photograph of the box, keeping the design as a whole from becoming too monochromatic. This also serves to heighten the viewer's awareness that this side of the composition is underwater.

Shells and underwater scenes of this type were produced from the late sixteenth to the seventeenth centuries. From early times, clam shells were used in *kai-awase* (shell matching), a game played by the aristocracy. These mollusks are also symbols of marital fidelity since the two halves of the bivalve must fit together perfectly.

The conch motif was introduced into Japanese culture as a Buddhist emblem. Conchs are also associated with the Japanese militant mountain priests known as *yamabushi*, who used them as signal horns. However, these rather simple objects were, like the clam, not very inspiring as an artistic subject, and their popularity, especially in lacquer, was short-lived. Artists who used this theme in later times usually depicted various mollusks as inlays within a much larger composition so that texture and color could be supplied by such materials as ivory and shell.

As is common to lacquers of high quality, as well as those created in earlier, more leisurely times, the composition shown here overflows from the lid to the base. Thus all visible surfaces are part of the whole design and can be enjoyed from any angle. The inside of the box is of *nashiji*.

CONNOISSEURSHIP: An interesting piece for study, authentically Kōdaiji in its styling. There is a large box in the Kōdaiji temple collection similar in design and composition to this one.

12

Document or scroll box (fubako)

A Kōdaiji-style box incorporating a geometric pattern decorated with scattered paulownia and chrysanthemum crests.

Momoyama period, late 16th century.
Dimensions: L 8 ⅝ in x W 2 ¼ in x H 2 in
(21.9 x 5.7 x 5.1 cm)

Covered boxes of this type, called *fubako,* were used for storage or transport of scroll paintings or of documents in the form of scrolls. The size of this particular piece suggests that its was probably used to store letters or other documents rather than paintings, which would have required a larger container.

Certain older design elements were revived in the Momoyama period, but they were often combined with new decorative themes. On this box the artist has incorporated the early Muromachi device known as *matsukawa-bishi*[12] (literally, "pine-bark diamonds"), a geometric division of space into lozenge shapes resembling the pattern of pine bark. On both the front and sides, the artist has cleverly used the angles inherent in the design to divide the various fields of the composition.

The seven flowers and grasses of autumn were an important motif in Japanese culture from early times, and the Heian aristocracy planted them in their gardens. A poem in the eighth-century imperial poetry anthology known as the *Man'yōshū* (8:1537-8), elicits the feeling of the season by itemizing each plant:

Aki no no ni	Flowers blossoming
sakitaru hana o	on autumn fields—
yubi orite	when I count them
kaki kazoureba	on my fingers,
nana kusa no hana	they number seven.
hagi ga hana	The flowers of bush clover,
obana kuzubana	pampas grass, and arrowroot;
nadeshiko no hana	pink,
ominaeshi	patrinia,
mata fujibakama	then mistflower and
asagao no hana	morning glory.[13]

These flowers and grasses became a favorite subject for decorative motifs on lacquers of the late sixteenth to early seventeenth century. The widow of the late-sixteenth-century hegemon Toyotomi Hideyoshi

bequeathed a group of lacquer objects strikingly decorated in this fashion to the temple Kōdaiji (see entry 11).

All seven of the flowers and grasses are not necessarily represented when alluding to this subject (and they are not all represented in the present box). In the Kōdaiji style, the theme might also accompany variations on the Toyotomi family *mon,* or crest. An alternate member of the seven flowers and grasses was the chrysanthemum, which was being utilized by the thirteenth century as the crest of the imperial family and is now the national flower of Japan. The scroll box shown here can be placed in front of the viewer in such a way that the long-stemmed chrysanthemums seem to grow up the length of the lid.[14]

On both the top and bottom sections, the geometry of the design acts as an arrow, calling attention to the bold pattern of the central section of the composition, where the prominent, jagged *matsukawa-bishi* is embossed with seven crests. Four of these employ the "five-and-seven" flower and leaf configuration of the paulownia that is the family crest of the Toyotomi. The other three contain chrysanthemum blossoms. Whether their use signifies a relationship to the imperial family, either as owner or giver of this scroll box, is unclear. Similar designs, in which these two *mon* are found together, have appeared on other lacquers of this period.[15] The interweaving of design elements and a variety of textures make this piece particularly effective.

Placing the box in front of the viewer as described above, and proceeding to the left as though reading a scroll, the members of the seven flowers and grasses of autumn that are represented here appear as follows:

Hagi (bush clover). This woody shrub with small, rounded leaves is considered the epitome of the seven. In season it bears delicate reddish purple flowers that grow along its arching branches. The autumn winds scatter its petals, and its seeds may be ground and eaten with a rice gruel.

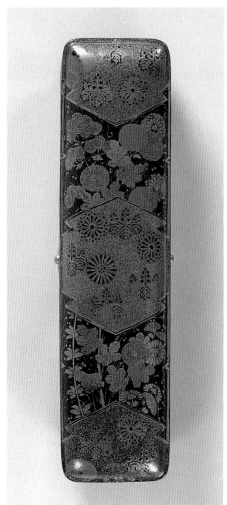

Above: overview of the box. Below left: the lid. Below right: detail of the lid.

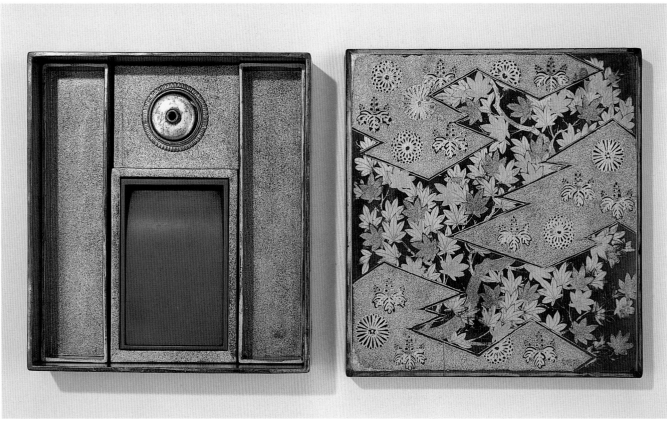

Above: detail of the right side, showing box and lid. Below: inkstone box from the Suntory Museum showing a similar matsukawa-bishi pattern.

Kikyō (Chinese bellflower, or morning glory). Its five-petaled, trumpet-shaped blossoms, ranging in color from pink and white to blue, appear in late summer to early fall.

Nadeshiko (fringed pink). It resembles a small carnation and grows in clusters of five.

Ominaeshi (*Patrinia scabiosaefolia,* sometimes referred to as "maiden flower"). Often shown in combination with *susuki.* Its tiny florets fan out to slightly arched, umbrellalike yellow sprays.

Continuing around to the other long side of the box, these flowers are repeated in a different order. The most interesting aspect of the design is its striking unification of fields of sharp angles with soft images. Another noteworthy object with the same pattern is a *suzuribako,* or inkstone box (see opposite), in the collection of the Suntory Museum in Tokyo.[16] The double gold and black striping edging the jagged geometric repeat in both boxes encloses a similar *nashiji* ground. Moreover, the techniques of *taka maki-e* employed to create the textured emblems are also identical.

CONNOISSEURSHIP: The worn condition of this box suggests centuries of use in the course of many trips. There are age cracks along the shoulders of the long sides, and parts of the surfaces are worn. In certain areas the finish is completely worn off. The side rings are a replacement, but they are so obviously of the wrong type that it is apparent that no effort was made to replicate the original. Moreover, this container shows little restoration. To a serious collector or a museum, this is as it should be. Too often the untrained, in their desire for perfection, forget that antiques can seldom be preserved in their original condition. Excessive or poor restoration can subvert the original intent of the artist.

13
Mirror box (kagamibako)

Chrysanthemums by the eastern fence.

Momoyama period, early 17th century.
Dimensions: DIA 5 ½ in x H 2 ¼ in
(13.9 x 5.7 cm)

The theme of chrysanthemums in bloom was one of the favorite subjects of lacquerers working in the Kōdaiji style. This mirror box displays an assortment of mature blossoms growing within a fencelike enclosure that can be seen on the sides of both lid and base. Sprays of pampas grass highlighted with dewdrops against the sectioned fence draw the eye to the lower level of the composition.

This box displays what may be referred to as a "frontal-projection" design: a flattened, two-dimensional image that originates at the base of the box and appears to grow upward, overflowing onto the lid and across its surface. This pictorial treatment echoes Muromachi conventions, but brings them to a new maturity. The complexity of the composition, with the fence rising along the circular sides in a zigzag pattern, as well as its contrasting proportions, are characteristic of the experimentation seen in lacquer designs of this period. The fence, executed in e-nashiji, stands out dramatically against the solid black ro-iro ground. This and the painterly quality of the pure gold lacquer are characteristic of the Kōami masters and their ateliers.

The theme of chrysanthemums growing by a fence, associated with an atmosphere of melancholy and withdrawal from the world, goes back to fourth-century China. It appears in a poem by the Chinese poet Tao Yuanming (365–427; also known as Tao Qian), who wrote, "I pick chrysanthemums by the eastern hedge / See the southern mountain, calm and still."[17] A thousand years later, literate Japanese found in such poems a sympathetic echo of their own despondency over the endless military conflicts of their era. This theme seems to have first appeared on Japanese lacquer boxes in the early Kamakura period. This mirror box is typical of those found in the set that was part of a bride's trousseau, but men of high station also often used mirrors when grooming their hair.

In typical Kōdaiji style, the blossoms, leaves, and fence are executed in e-nashiji, which includes the addition of the orange-colored additive known as gamboge. The tinted tonal shading makes the flaked gold suspended in the lacquer appear richer in color. To further emphasize the leaf pattern, veining and general outlining have been applied in a variation on the low-relief technique called keuchi, and the the floral design as a whole stands out in dramatic low relief against the plain black background. The chrysanthemum blossoms and leaves are made of fine gold and silver powders combined with flaked gold of different sizes. The black lines that define the shapes within the gold pictures are left in reserve, a difficult and painstaking technique. The strewn powders used to make the blossoms have not been given a final protective coat, but have been "left as sprinkled" (maki-hanashi). The absence of a covering coat has allowed the silver to oxidize considerably.

The weave of the fabric used to line the entire box is visible through the lacquer coating on the inner surface of the lid.

CONNOISSEURSHIP: The design, style, and techniques employed in the composition of a piece all help in reaching conclusions as to artist, date, and authenticity. This box employs typical Kōdaiji techniques and styling. Despite the fact that the workmanship of the interior is not as fine as that of the exterior, there is little doubt that this piece is by a Kōami. The exquisite craftsmanship evident in the design and finish could only have been conceived and executed by a skilled, well-trained, and highly imaginative artist. The outlining of all veins and edges in unadulterated gold powder is not common to this style, as it required more time and expense than standard pieces. This was probably a special order for an aristocratic male patron of refined taste.

Above: overview of the box. Below: interior of the lid.

14
Storage box for combs (kushibako)

Decorated with flowering clematis.

Edo period, first half of 17th century.
Dimensions: L 6 ¾ in x W 5 ¾ in x H 5 ⅜ in
(17.2 x 14.6 x 13.7 cm)

Bulky, squarish boxes of this general size, with a fitted inner tray, were used for storage of a woman's combs.

Intertwining tendrils of the flowering six-petaled clematis vine are shown, and its blossoms appear on all the surfaces of this dramatically designed box, in typical early-seventeenth-century style. The soft contour of the underlying form is emphasized by the way in which the growing plant gently encircles the sides of the lid and the base. The surface ground of the box is of a rich black *ro-iro*, which dramatizes the flowers, vines, and leaf formations of finely sprinkled gold powders in the low-relief (*hira maki-e*). *E-nashiji*, with its orange color, is used for contrast within the petals, and the *kakiwari* technique of scratching the surface design away with a sharp instrument allows the underground black to be used as the veining within the leaves.[18]

A great deal of thought went into the design of this box, and the execution is flawless. For example, vines and leaves also encircle the high, deep inner panels of its inside lower section, where they continue their circle of growth. There they gradually diminish in size until only a tiny, thin tendril is left, suggesting further growth to come.

The deep, overlapping lid has a typical trilobed cutaway on each of its long sides. This cutout allows the lid to be lifted easily and also accommodates two circular metal side attachments. These hold movable rings, through which woven silk tie cords can be passed and then joined in a bow, thus securing the lid. In this example the metal side pieces are decorated with the "three-and-five" floral *kiri mon*, or paulownia crest, typically associated with the Toyotomi family. The gold wash that coated these attachments at one time has been worn away. The inner fitted tray, which rests on an inside ledge in the box, is of a deep, shiny black *ro-iro* with matte gold edging.

CONNOISSEURSHIP: Most large boxes for storing combs were made from the seventeenth to the middle of the eighteenth century, after which their popularity diminished. Almost all extant examples originated from this period.

15
Tiered incense container (jūkōgō)

Decorated with two cranes, a mantled turtle
(*minogame*), a pine tree, and bamboo.

Edo period, 17th century.
Dimensions: DIA 2 ⅛ in x H 2 ¹⁵⁄₁₆ in
(5.4 x 7.5 cm)

This piece is part of an elaborate set of articles used in the incense game (see entry 49). The longevity symbols of pine, crane, and turtle or tortoise were a favorite theme on boxes until the early part of the eighteenth century. The frontal-projection approach to the handling of the images seen here, in which the artist uses the whole surface of the box for decoration, is one example of the Japanese concept of total composition. The ground is of a very high quality *ro-iro*, and the rest of this lacquer painting is in *fundame*, with *e-nashiji* used to fill in the central sections of the bamboo leaves. The painterly approach apparent here displays a flexibility in composition that contrasts with the stiffer designs of earlier periods. The techniques applied range from true *hira maki-e* to small amounts of *taka maki-e*. *Keuchi* has been added to further emphasize those areas that include *e-nashiji*.

This tiered incense container consists of three sections and a cover. The bottom section (*hiuchi*), is lined with metal to hold the ash on which the incense is burned, while the middle tier was designed to contain mica chips on which the incense may be nested. The top section held incense in the form of pieces of aromatic wood.

The quality of the lacquer on this piece is extremely good, and the theme dramatically executed. The interiors of the tiers not lined in metal are made of the highest quality *ro-iro*.

CONNOISSEURSHIP: The loose feeling of the design in such a compact space speaks more of an individual artist than an atelier. To date, little information has been published about seventeenth-century lacquers in general, with the exception of a recent work on Kōdaiji objects and their techniques. Patronage of this type of work was still dependent on the samurai class, as merchant-class sponsorship did not emerge until about the second half of the century.

16

Incense container (kōgō)

A portable Chinese chest (karabitsu) rests on the earth among thickly scattered ivy vines and leaves.

Edo period, 17th century.
Dimensions: L 2 ⅞ in x W 2 ⅛ in x H 1 in
(7.3 x 5.4 x 2.5 cm)

The decorations on this box allude both directly and indirectly to an episode in the tenth-century *Ise monogatari*, or *Tales of Ise*, a classic of Japanese literature. *Tales of Ise* comprises 125 episodes, each of which consists of a group of poems embedded in a prose narrative that tells how the poems came to be written. It is commonly assumed to be loosely based on the life of the Heian nobleman and poet Ariwara no Narihira (825–80), the author of many of the poems included in the text.[19]

In the episode alluded to here, a young nobleman, forced by unhappy circumstances to leave the capital, sets out with his companions on a journey to the eastern provinces, where he hopes to find a new life. They reach a point in the journey called Yatsuhashi or "Eight Bridges," so named because of a complex system of plank bridges that crosses over a marshland. While resting at the edge of the marsh, they notice the deep purple irises blooming there, in striking contrast to the muddy waters. Sad and homesick, the hero of the story composes a type of acrostic poem, in which the initial syllables of its five lines, as written in Japanese, spell out *"ka-ki-tsu-ba-ta,"* the Japanese name of the flower:

Karagoromo	I have a beloved wife,
Kitsutsu narenishi	Familiar as the skirt
Tsuma shi areba	Of a well-worn robe,
Harubaru kinuru	And so this distant journeying
Tabi o shi zo omou	Fills my heart with grief.[20]

This scene, and the poem, became one of the most famous in Japanese literature, and by the Edo period the images were so ingrained as a symbol of the episode that only the flowers and the planked bridge were necessary to recall it.

As they continue on their way, the travelers enter a lane overgrown with ivy, where they meet a traveling priest. Because they know him, they give the priest a message to carry home. Thus it is that the subject of the box's lid—a *karabitsu*, or elegant portable case for scriptures that was often carried by Buddhist priests—alludes indirectly to this literary episode. Its curved shoulder straps seem to be caught in some silent movement, and vines and leaves surrounding it suggest an image with poetic overtones rather than that of an everyday object. The *karabitsu* is shown nestled among masses of leaves that cover all the surfaces of the box: its top, four sides, and even the bottom.

A more direct reference to the episode from the *Tales of Ise* is revealed when the box is opened and the lid is placed to its right, side by side, with the inner surface up. Together the two pieces form a unified composition, complete with poetic inscription. Summer irises and grasses surround an eight-planked bridge. The poem quoted above is inscribed on the surfaces of the planks in the flowing Japanese script known as *kana*.

CONNOISSEURSHIP: The quality of the box is reinforced by the continuous design of flowing leaves that covers not only its lid and four sides, but flows across the unseen bottom surface as well. The gold *maki-e* methods of *e-nashiji*, *harigaki*, and *hira maki-e* on a black ground are simply, elegantly, and carefully executed, and the combined use of these techniques also helps to date the piece.

Above: exteriors of the lid and the bottom of the box. Below: interiors of the box and lid.

17
Inkstone box (suzuribako)

Chrysanthemums at night in full bloom.

Edo period, 17th century.
Dimensions: L 9 in x W 8 ¼ in x H 1 ⅞ in
(22.9 x 20.9 x 4.8 cm)

The comparatively rare inverted corners (iri-zumi) of this box demanded more time and attention on the part of the craftsman than the usual right-angled ones, and signal that this is a special object. A specialist in this form would have been necessary for its construction, as the inner trays must also conform to the irregular shape. Lacquer boxes of this kind are therefore usually of high quality.

The blooming chrysanthemums and their leaves have been flawlessly executed in the difficult technique known as togidashi maki-e. The simple elegance of the result belies the artistry necessary to achieve it—involving a slow buildup of layers of lacquer, with careful polishing after each application, until a final polish at last reveals the underlying design. Of particular importance is the subtle and careful use of the stone and charcoal that are the implements required for polishing and finishing the final stages of togidashi.

Only two colors and gold powder sufficed to achieve the extraordinary effect seen on this box. After the black ground was finished and dried, a thin layer of gold powder was applied in the shape of the design. A transfer sheet of the drawing was then laid down to give the artist an outline for the picture. Thick gold powder was sprinkled on, section by section, until complete. Then a thin coat of clear lacquer was added to "fix" this layer so that the powder would not exfoliate during the drying process. Each petal, flower, and stem was slowly and carefully drawn on this surface in a sienna-colored lacquer. While this underpainting was still wet, gold powders were sprinkled on it, and allowed to dry. Again a coat of clear lacquer was used as a fixative. Section by section, the artist continued his work until the complete image had been laid in. Finally the entire surface was given the additional coats of lacquer required to make the surface even. Only an expert in this technique knows how many layers must be added to complete the entire work prior to the final polishing that reveals, on the same level, the gold drawing of the composition. In this particular example the skill demonstrated is even more remarkable since the design overflows onto the edge of the left side of the lid.

The inner construction of this box is quite unusual. Typically, inner trays rest on the floor of the bottom section in a close fit. Here, however, two elevated brackets attached to both sides in the basic underconstuction of the box allow all the internal components to rest suspended above the floor of the box.

In the center section of the base the fluted water dropper and the unusually contoured inkstone, edged in gold powder, complete what appears as a simple arrangement. The two end trays are slightly uneven in size, adding a touch of individuality.

CONNOISSEURSHIP: This box is an example of extraordinary artistry, technique, and construction. Knowing that the flowers represented on this box will soon loose their petals and die with the approach of winter, one senses the poet's meaning:

Toritomuru	Because there was no
Mono ni shi araneba	Way to seize and hold
Toshi tsuki o	The swift moving months and years of life,
Aware ana u to	In delight and sorrow
Sugushitsuru kana	I have passed them carelessly.[21]

Above: exterior of the lid. Below: interiors of the box and lid.

18

Inkstone box (suzuribako)

A pair of hares frolic among autumn grasses.

Edo period, late 16th or early 17th century.
Dimensions: L 10 ¾ in x W 8 ⅝ in x H 1 ⅞ in
(27.3 X 21.9 X 4.8 cm)

This box was designed by Hon'ami Kōetsu (1558–1637), the celebrated artist, calligrapher, and designer of ceramics and lacquerware. In 1615 Kōetsu founded an artistic community at Takagamine, a village near Kyoto. He attracted suitable followers and was shortly joined by the equally famous painter-calligrapher, Tawaraya Sōtatsu (died ca 1643). Sōtatsu, a major artist in his own right, joined Kōetsu in producing gorgeous and freshly decorative works of art.

In lacquer, Kōetsu devised new forms, subject matter, and techniques. The addition of imposing lead inlays, usually against or in combination with a gold-lacquer ground, became his hallmark. The massiveness of his domed-lid inkstone boxes contrasted with their delicate poetic overtones and elegant forms to define an unusual, innovative style. Large, isolated figures of men or animals, or symbolic depictions of famous places, accompanied by poetry, were treated in a new "close-up" approach.

Kōetsu made few lacquer objects and he did not usually sign his pieces; however, his work is unmistakable. It is not known whether he lacquered the objects himself or merely supplied the design and oversaw their manufacture. The latter is probably true.

The shape of this thick-edged box, with its tricorner bevel topping a flat undersurface, is unusual and so far found only on boxes attributed to Kōetsu.[22] In the middle of its top surface are two large, long-eared hares viewed from the rear. Created from a layer of lead foil placed over under-contours of *sabi urushi*, the two form a tight but fluid composition with their rounded haunches, superbly contoured paws, and long, jutting ears.

On a black lacquer ground that has lightened considerably, they seem to be burrowing their way through a field of pampas grass and clusters of *ominaeshi*, or "maiden flowers." These plants display part of the red underpainting used in preparation of the sprinkled gold, most of which has since flaked off.

The inside of the inkstone box follows Kōetsu's usual approach. A plain rectangular copper water dropper sits inside a single fitted tray, along with, and directly above, the softly contoured inkstone. Pampas grasses, painted before the two accoutrements were inserted, add color and a sense of movement to the setting. The inside of the lid echoes the theme of the bottom section, with the addition of a three-quarter moon in characteristic lead overlay for color and texture.

CONNOISSEURSHIP: This is a rare example of Kōetsu's work. Judging from the considerable wear on all its surfaces its owner must have used it often.

Above: exterior of the lid. Below left: interiors of the box and lid.
Below right: interior of the box with the inkstone and water dropper removed.

19
Storage box for sweets (kashibako)

Decorated with a large isolated image of an aristocrat's carriage.

Edo period, 17th century.
Dimensions: L 11 ¾ in x W 9 in x H 2 ¼ in
(29.9 x 22.9 x 5.7 cm)

The subject matter, shape, and look of this box, as well as the absence of the side rings usually found on a document storage container, make it likely that it was designed to store the sweets used in the tea ceremony. Here *rantai shikki*, or bamboo basketry work, is beautified with inlay and lacquer decoration, lending the surface texture and depth. The presentation of a large, single image—in this case an aristocrat's carriage—encompassing most of the surface is typical of Hon'ami Kōetsu's style.

The type of ox-drawn carriage depicted, with attendants on either side, was used by the Kyoto nobility of the Heian period. Here, the vehicle is an allusion to the fourth chapter of the classic Heian-period novel *The Tale of Genji*. Entitled "Yūgao," this chapter tells the story of Prince Genji's seduction of a fragile and innocent lady, whom he takes in his carriage to a deserted house, where they spend the night. In the morning he discovers that she has died, apparently having been attacked by the jealous spirit of one of Genji's other mistresses. After holding a secret funeral, Genji is stricken ill and does not recover until months later, in the autumn.

This episode, like many others in *The Tale of Genji*, became so famous that only a symbol, in this case the carriage, was needed to remind the viewer of the specific episode that was being alluded to. The poignancy of the theme made it so popular that it became a favorite subject for decorating lacquer objects associated with the incense ceremony.

The rustic appearance of this box conforms with the seventeenth-century aesthetic known as *wabi*. The interior of both top and bottom have been well coated with black lacquer as a sealant. The inner surface of the lid has been simply finished with the insertion of a harvest moon and a few sprigs of autumn grass. The inner surface of the base is also decorated, but again in the form of only a few blades of pampas grass, symbolizing autumn, rendered in sprinkled gold powder.

This piece is an odd mixture of precision and near crudity. Most of the carriage is made of a sheet of lead cut to size and applied as an overlay. The long sashes, where the lady's sleeves would rest, and the curtains are in gold *fundame*, and the crossbars that hold the carriage's adjustable bamboo curtain are made of inlaid pieces of rather roughly finished mother-of-pearl. Although some parts of the carriage are rather crudely executed, the wheel is perfectly formed. The sections between the spokes are cut out and applied very carefully, and the components of the wheel fit well. The detailing of the slat work is extremely fine, as is that of the bracing the passenger would have used to step down from the carriage.

The sheet lead was applied to basketweave for the sake of contrast and dramatic effect, but without much thought for the work's durability. Metal expands and shrinks with changes in temperature, while unsealed basketwork shrinks permanently. As a result, the metal overlay has tended to separate from the undercoating of the basket-woven base. All the metal parts, however, were coated with lacquer to protect them from the air and prevent oxidation.

CONNOISSEURSHIP: The contrast between the fine drawing in gold on the slatted curtains and the almost primitive crudeness of the inlays dates the piece to the seventeenth century and suggests an artist out of the Kyoto mainstream. In its day, this must have been a very daring composition, but time and the elements have blunted its effect. A subtle edging of wood is now visible under the moon inlay, revealing the underlying construction.

Above: exterior of the lid. Below: interiors of the box and lid.

20

Inkstone box (suzuribako)

Decorated with a single reclining deer gazing into
the distance.

Edo period, mid-17th century.
Dimensions: L 8 ⅛ in x W 4 ½ in x H 1 ¼ in
(20.7 X 11.4 X 3.2 cm)

Executed in the style of Hon'ami Kōetsu, this
box shows a solitary deer resting on a mound
of earth. Most of the composition is supplied
by the natural graining of the underlying cryptomeria
wood, which suggests distant hills and mountains. In
the foreground, small bamboo leaves cover part of the
deer's body, which is composed of layered lead sheeting,
while the bamboo is rendered in subdued matte
gold *fundame*.

The reclining deer is silhouetted against a gold
and brown background. Its antlers are inlaid in dark
gray mother-of-pearl with a slight green highlight.
The inner part of the lid shows a three-quarter moon
fashioned of the same material as the deer's body. To
suggest night, the artist has chosen a black lacquer
ground. The slim, rectangular inkstone is surmounted
by a plain water dropper. Chinese Buddhist cloud
designs, with a few small patches of grass in plain flat
gold, are the only additional lacquer decorations.

Each symbol has its own significance. A few lines,
and water may be imagined. The autumn moon, peeking
through a leafless branch of an unseen tree, echoes
the theme of fall, a season associated with loneliness,
and one that appeals to poetic Japanese sensibilities.
The following poem aptly expresses the mood evoked
by the lid of this box:

Okuyama ni	Treading through the
Momiji fumiwake	Autumn leaves in the
	deepest mountains
Naku shika no	I hear the belling
Koe kiku toki zo	of the lonely deer—
Aki wa kanashiki	Then it is that autumn is
	sad[23]

The box was evidently designed to express the *wabi*
esthetic of the tea ceremony.

CONNOISSEURSHIP: The deer's body is probably of lead
sheeting molded over a contour of *sabi urushi*, but only
analysis of its composition can confirm this. The natural
graining of the cryptomeria wood used as a ground
suggests crevices and distant hills, giving a sense of
depth that cannot be achieved with applied decoration.

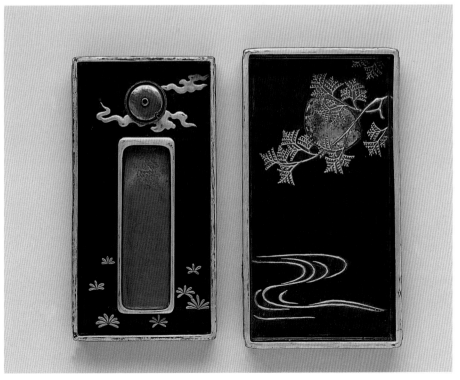

Above: exterior of the lid. Below: interiors of the box and lid.

21

Incense container (kōgō)

Decorated with pea pods, vines, and foliage.

Edo period, late 17th or early 18th century.
Dimensions: DIA 3 %16 in X H 1 ⅛ in
(9.0 X 2.9 cm)

This box was designed by either Ogata Kōrin (1658–1716) or one of his close disciples. Kōrin, who was born after Hon'ami Kōetsu's death, was Kōetsu's major follower. Perhaps Kōetsu's broad, stark designs in lacquer appealed to only a few, since only a few extant objects are attributed to him. The name "Rimpa" is used to refer to the paintings and lacquers produced by Kōetsu, Tawaraya Sōtatsu, Kōrin and a few of their later followers. It derives from the *rin* of "Kōrin" and the word *ha,* meaning "school." The multitalented Kōrin, who modified Kōetsu's highly innovative, massive inlays with a more delicate sense of design and decorative quality, helped the Rimpa school carry on the tradition he so admired. However, like his "teacher" he did not usually sign his lacquers. Therefore it is questionable whether he actually made the boxes himself, or if, like Kōetsu, he only supplied the designs and oversaw the work. In any event, the Kōrin style of lacquer is distinctive, and this box is typical of the designs and complex combinations of techniques and materials that he created.

During Kōrin's time realism entered the mainstream of Japanese art, as stylization gave way to a careful study of nature. The domed top of this *kōgō* is compactly designed. Inlays of textured lead, contoured in the bulky shapes of pea pods, have been applied over *sabi urushi.* These are interwoven with the raised forms of leaves and vines, which are covered in sprinkled gold. The design of this piece would have called for elaborate sketching and careful instructions, as each layer of material had to be applied in a particular order. This is an extremely complex, multitextured composition, which overlaps to include the sharp curve that carries the imagery to the bottom section. Thick mother-of-pearl pieces form the leaves and buds. *Fundame,* a matte gold technique that was used more often as a backdrop effect until around the late eighteenth century, provides a muted ground. The interior is made of the same ground as the surface.

CONNOISSEURSHIP: It required great skill in lacquering to achieve a clean and continuous design over the sharp curve of the lid, despite interruption by inlays and the use of a variety of lacquer techniques. Nevertheless it seems unlikely that Kōrin himself was directly involved in the lacquering process. Because *urushi* is highly allergenic, constant exposure to it is necessary to become and remain desensitized. A lacquer master starts young, and by in effect "eating it" every day whenever he wets the point of a brush in his mouth, maintains his immunity to it. Indeed, *urushi* is so allergenic that many wives of living artists tell of getting lacquer "poisoning" (an allergic reaction) when washing their husbands' socks. Therefore it is doubtful that either Kōetsu or Kōrin, both of whom were principally painters, would have been able to work directly with *urushi.*

22

Inkstone box (suzuribako)

Decorated with a geometric pattern of medallions showing a hare leaping over water against a background of lotuses in bloom.

Edo period, late 17th century.
Dimensions: L 8 ⅞ in x w 8 ¼ in x H 1 ⁹⁄₁₆ in
(22.6 x 20.9 x 3.9 cm)

The design on this box is probably based on one by Ogata Kōrin. The identical units in the medallion pattern suggest the use of a stencil similar to that utilized in textile designs. In this case, two separate waxed-paper cutouts would have been needed: one for the medallion containing the right-facing hare against a background of lotus leaves and blossoms viewed from the side; the other for the medallion with the left-facing hare and the lotus blossoms viewed head on.[24] These two patterns are alternated across the top, bottom, and all four sides of the box.

The large inkstone and square bronze water dropper decorated with a chrysanthemum are original to the box.

The picture on the inside of the lid refers to a well-known Chinese legend about a woodcutter who, while wandering through the forest one day, discovered a cave where two men (later revealed as Taoist immortals) were playing the board game known in Japanese as *go*. He was so entranced by their game that he became oblivious to the passing of time. After what seemed only a short interval, the players suggested that he leave. When he moved to pick up his ax, it disintegrated at his touch, and upon returning home he found that many centuries had passed.

The lotus blossoms on the exterior of the lid are associated with purity of mind, and the hares with the moon and thus the passage of time. The image decorating the inside of the lid shows the *go* board in play. The ax rests under the board, and scattered petals also represent the passing of time.

The *go* board has been textured in a variation of the technique known as *mokume*, in which wood grain is simulated in a stylized pattern. The lines on the board have been drawn in black lacquer against the pure darkened silver of its surface. Delicate blossoms with tiny stamens of gold in *hira maki-e* are scattered on the board's surface and around its base. The legs supporting the board are of gold *fundame*. The delicate use of silver, only slightly highlighted with the application of a subdued gold, lends the design a quiet dignity.

Knowing the story behind the symbols is part of the enjoyment of Japanese art. In the process of understanding and interpreting them, all the senses are stimulated and the mind roams freely. This box may have been made as a memento of a special event, or perhaps the owner was a man of philosophical spirit.

CONNOISSEURSHIP: Kōrin was an expert in textile design, so it would have been natural for him to incorporate into lacquers the use of a stencil to create a repeat pattern. Other lacquer makers of the time, such as Yamamoto Shunshō (1610–82) and his sons, who were masters of the *togidashi* technique, concentrated on reproducing the subject matter seen in the woodblock prints of the period.

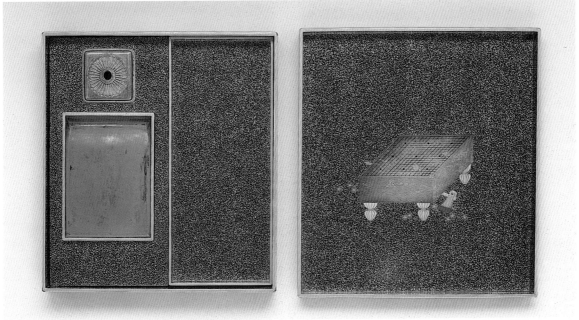

Above: exterior of the lid. Below: interiors of the box and lid.

23
Portable lunch box set
(sagejūbako)

Decorated with a variety of motifs and
figurative scenes.

Edo period, 18th century.
Dimensions: L 10 in x W 5 ½ in x H 9 ¾ in
(25.4 X 13.9 X 24.8 cm)

Portable lunch box sets like this one became
popular in the early Edo period, when people
started eating a third meal between breakfast
and dinner. The set, called a *sagejūbako*, typically consisted of a handled carrying case with a separate section for two containers of *sake*; an open container for
food; a serving plate; and a set of three to five tiered
boxes with a lid, called a *jūbako*. The *jūbako* in the lunch
kit shown here has four boxes.

The carrying case. The upper surface of the carrying
case is decorated with a group of *minogame*, or "mantled turtles." Shown playing among plantains in
flowing water, they have been made into fantasy creatures with large feet, sharp claws, and fierce faces with
glaring eyes resembling a dragon's. The design on each
of their shells is different but their facial expressions
are similar.

The jūbako. The lid of the set of tiered boxes shows
a small village with a farmer gazing up at the almost
cloudless sky. The square boxes making up the set fit
tightly on top of one another to preserve the freshness
and contain the odor of the foods stored within. Each
box is deeper than the one above it, with the deepest
on the bottom.

Alternating patterns decorate all four sides of each
tier. The second and fourth boxes (numbering from
the top) have black *togidashi* backgrounds with heavy
floral scrollwork and a variation of color achieved
through the use of *nashiji*, silver inlay, and gold *hira
maki-e* with some *keuchi*. The designs, reminiscent of
textile patterns, are full of movement. The first and
third tiers, on the other hand, have panels set in
oblong reserves, decorated with pictures of birds, fish,
and animals. All the lacquering is done in *togidashi*,
using gold and *aokin* (gold with an admixture of silver),
carefully shaded and very expertly executed.

The *jūbako* fits into a cutout on the partition that
separates it from a small uncovered dish that rests on
the very bottom of the carrier. The decoration of this
dish, of grapes finished in *nashiji*, suggests that it was
used for serving sweets.

The two sake containers. Each side of the square *sake*
bottles has a decorative panel illustrating a poetic or
philosophical theme. On one bottle the front panel
shows a bird perched on a *torii*, the gate marking the
entrance to a Shinto shrine. The remaining three panels bear human figures: a sage, a Buddhist monk, and a
weary traveler. All are depicted as insignificant figures
compared to the grandeur of the natural world in the
form of an expansive night sky with clouds lit softly
by a distant moon. The clouds and moon are rendered
in a light sprinkling of silver and gold powders, while
the rest of the images, also in *togidashi*, are formed of
either plain gold or a mixed silver and gold particles.

The other *sake* container has one panel with a
Chinese sage and his porter, who points to the distant
mountains. In the second panel, a monkey looks down
into the water, which reflects the moon and the mountains at his back. In a third, a bird stands eating, and
the fourth side shows two hares, one in gold, the other
in silver. All scenes are executed in *togidashi*. Distant
mountains appear in the background of all four scenes
on this bottle, once again suggesting the presence and
dominance of nature.

Both the subject matter and the style of painting
on these two containers would have served their owner
and his guests as a source for philosophical discourse
as their contents were being consumed.

CONNOISSEURSHIP: With the exception of a square
tray set in its own compartment above the tiered
boxes, all the components of this ensemble match.
Pieces were often lost from beloved possessions such
as this, and replacements either found or specially
made. Here another tray, not particularly appropriate
to the themes presented or the techniques employed
in the rest of the set, has been substituted for the lost
original.

Above: the set packed in its carrying case. Below: the set with its elements disassembled.

Opposite page: detail of the first and second tiers of the jūbako. Above: top of the carrying case. Below: views of three sides of the jūbako.

24
Document box (ryōshibako)

Decorated with a fish-shaped gong, two volumes of Buddhist scripture, and a ritual implement known as a *vajra*.

Edo period, late 17th or early 18th century.
Dimensions: L 10 in x W 8 ¾ in x H 3 ½ in
(25.4 x 22.2 x 8.9 cm)

The celebrated artist and poet Ogawa Haritsu (1663–1747) made this box, as is indicated by the raised characters in seal script (*tensho*) across the surface of the gong reading Mūchūan (literally, "hermitage amid dreams"), one of his sobriquets.

Born into a samurai family in Kyōto[25], Haritsu, popularly known as Ritsuō, was a devout Buddhist who mastered Kanō school painting, poetry (particularly *haikai*) and other forms of literature, the tea ceremony, and flower arrangement. Like other artists of the Genroku era (1688–1703) he benefited from a flourishing of the arts stimulated by the increasing patronage of a strong and growing middle class. In lacquer, free thinkers practiced innovation, explored brilliance in color, and introduced a diversity of techniques and subject matter. Among Genroku artists Haritsu was a blend of the best the culture could produce. His training as a potter (see entry 25) is evident in his ceramic inlays, an element almost always incorporated into his lacquers.

The body of the fish-shaped gong on the lid of this box was made of *sabi urushi*, a mixture of lacquer and another substance providing bulk, such as powdered pumice. The surface of the resulting molded shape was then finished in various techniques, replicating the appearance of iron.

The two books under the gong are decorated in *nashiji*, a technique in which sprinkled gold particles are embedded in a transparent orange-tinted lacquer. Here the effect is like an orange sky glittering with gilded stars. The title visible on the uppermost of the two volumes indicates that it is a sutra dealing with self-examination, an integral concept in many sects of Buddhism.

The scepterlike object lying under the head of the fish is a ritual implement known in Sanskrit as a *vajra* (*kongōsho* in Japanese), a stylized thunderbolt wielded by practitioners of esoteric Buddhism as a symbolic weapon against illusions, passions, and earthly desires. The *vajra* was first contoured in *sabi urushi*, then covered with black lacquer and gilded sparingly, allowing the black and gold to blend harmoniously. Considering Haritsu's religious attitudes, it seems natural that this holy symbol would be thus fashioned in a traditional medium, using traditional techniques.

The rope from which the gong would be suspended is treated quite differently. Here, Haritsu employed a contrasting inlay of tortoiseshell, a material noted for its muted color and smooth texture. The subtle use of different materials and color combinations displayed on this box epitomizes Haritsu's constant attention to contrast and balance within his compositions.

The inside of the lid is a study in contrasting materials and design elements that also reflect Haritsu's contemplative nature. Here a ceramic inlay in the form of a lotus petal is set against a jagged lotus leaf rendered as a broad mass of lead-colored lacquer. The striated petal has been carefully glazed in shades of pink and white to duplicate the tonal variation of a living flower. Its curved and falling form expresses a single instant in its existence as it floats downward to some final resting place. At the extreme right of the composition, two long stems run in close parallel to the edge of the lid, providing a strong vertical momentum. One of them terminates in a lotus pod, seen from the side, and executed in muted gold *taka maki-e* and *hira maki-e*. All the decoration on the lid's interior evokes images of late fall and approaching winter.

CONNOISSEURSHIP: Iron particles in the black lacquer have oxidized, causing what is termed caramelization. The change in color resulting from this chemical reaction helps date the box, while at the same time providing a soft, contrasting background. Such fading is usually not even, and the random alteration in tone indicates the quality of the iron filings used to create the black in the lacquer.

Above: exterior of the lid. Below left: interior of the lid. Below right: detail of the exterior of the lid.

25

Inkstone box (suzuribako)

An unusual oval box with a deep overlapping lid, completely covered in the *tsugaru nuri* technique.

Edo period, early 18th century.
Dimensions: L 13 ½ in x W 10 in x H 2 in
(34.3 X 25.4 X 5.1 cm)

This box, like the one in entry 24, was made by Ogawa Haritsu. The colorful lid is of *tsugaru nuri*, a technique perfected in the castle town of Hirosaki in the Tsugaru region of what is now Aomori Prefecture.

The inventor of *tsugaru nuri* is said to have been Ikeda Gentarō, who is thought to have produced the first examples in 1686.[26] To create its mottled effect, a thick, uneven base of either *shibo urushi* (lacquer thickened with a stiffening agent) or *sabi urushi* was added to a black lacquer background, possibly with a spatula. Once dry, the surface was polished, red lacquer and silver powders were added, and a layer of brownish-yellow lacquer applied. When the lacquer was semi-dry, mother-of-pearl was sprinkled on in what may appear a random pattern. Then the artist carefully scraped away certain parts of the lacquer with a small tool, creating a swirling pattern and revealing the black ground. After smoothing down the entire surface, he applied the final coats of clear lacquer.[27]

Ogawa Haritsu spent most of the last two decades of his life in the Tsugaru region, where he worked under the patronage of the local daimyo. Here he could select the best materials, experiment with new concepts, and express his ideas in different media. His experience in lacquer must have already been extraordinary in order for him to produce the objects that are extant. According to one source, he had studied lacquering under a Chinese master who visited Japan in the Genroku period (1688–1704).[28] This seems probable, since Chinese Ming and Qing lacquerers had already perfected the inlay techniques that appear in Haritsu's work. In any case, he used lacquer techniques that had never before been seen in Japan.

In about 1650, the celebrated Kyoto potter Nonomura Ninsei introduced colored overglaze enamels to earthenware pottery.[29] The buff-colored base clay found in the Kyoto area fired at only about eight or nine hundred degrees to produce an excellent example of what is termed faience. The fine crackle on the surface of this type of ceramic results from the different rates of expansion of the glaze and the underlying clay. Haritsu used both pottery and porcelain inlays in his lacquerwork , and employed Kyoto-type clay to achieve the same type of crackling effect.

The box shown here is oval, with a lid that overlaps the base almost completely. The scene on the exterior of the lid is framed at the left and top by the sparse branches and blossoms of a flowering plum tree. Within this subtle arch stands the Chinese Taoist immortal, Wang Gong (known also as Wang Qiao and, in Japanese, as Ōkyō), accompanied by a crane. Both look fondly down upon a small Chinese boy, who is examining an empty flower pot.

The sage's robe is an inlay covered in various shades of moss-green and umber lacquer. The faces and hands of both human figures as well as the exquisitely finished plum blossoms are in a cream-colored faience covered with a crackled glaze similar to that of Nonomura Ninsei. The crane is of white porcelain, covered with a clear glaze with a greenish cast similar to that seen on Hirado ware. The features of the immortal, the tail feathers of the bird, and the hair and face of the child are detailed in black lacquer.

The interior of box and lid are in black lacquer that has caramelized to a deep uneven brown. Any fittings it might have had are missing. Inside the lid, however, there is an inscription in Chinese, followed by a date, the artist's signature, and two green, square ceramic seals. The translation of the inscription is as follows:

> Plum blossoms are clean,
>   like the legendary *fu* blossoms,
> As pure as a gentle breeze above the cloud.
> Even Wang Gong, reckoned among
>   the divinities and immortals,
> Looks faded beside them.
> Plum blossoms bloom
>   like a white-robed immortal at Nian.[30]

Exterior of the lid.

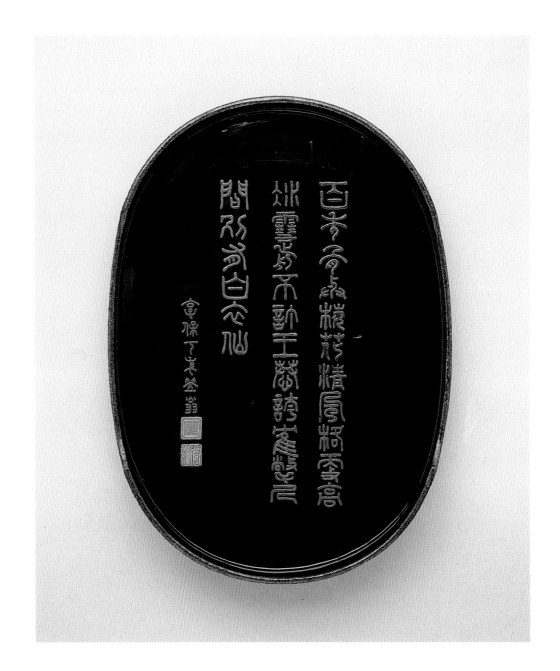

Interior of the lid.

The dated signature reads "Kyōhō *hinoto hitsuji,* Ritsuō." Kyōhō was the imperial reign title of the period 1716–35, while *hinoto hitsuji* refers to the specific year, given in the Chinese system of notation in use in Japan at that time[31], corresponding to 1727 in the Western calendar. The signature Ritsuō is one of the sobriquets used by Haritsu. The uppermost of the two green seals reads "Kan" and the lower one "Naoyuki," both being alternate names for the artist.

Wang Gong, the Chinese immortal depicted on the cover of the box and mentioned in the inscription, is referred to in many Chinese legends. In one, he wears a robe made of crane feathers. In another, he rides on a white crane, a celebrated symbol of longevity in Chinese mythology.

CONNOISSEURSHIP: Inscriptions, like the one in Chinese on this box, are especially difficult to render in lacquer. The seal script used here, derived from ancient Chinese models, would have been used and understood only by the well-educated of the time, and today few Japanese can read this style of script.

26

Inkstone box (suzuribako)

The lid is decorated with a sprig of hydrangea, a
lined piece of fabric, and a Chinese-style hand mirror
(*kagami*).

Edo period, 18th century.
Dimensions: L 12 ⅜ in x W 11 in x H 2 ¼ in
(31.5 x 27.9 x 5.7 cm)

Hydrangea (*ajisai*) blossoms like the one on
this box are extremely rare as a motif in lacquer. This is surprising, for the flower is
native to Japan and can be found in poetry as far back
as the eighth-century poetic anthology *Man'yōshu*. One
indication of its popularity is the existence, in
Kamakura, of a temple nicknamed the Ajisaidera, or
"hydrangea temple," which is celebrated for the beauty of its blossoms, particularly at their height during
the rainy season in late spring.

The undulating piece of lined silk is displayed primarily with its underside showing, which usually suggests intimacy. What little pattern is visible appears to
be decorated with a five-petaled flower.

This elegant cloth probably covered the third
object shown, a metal Chinese-style hand mirror
(*kagami*), which was used by samurai as they dressed
their hair. During the Edo period men rather than
women utilized mirrors with this simple rounded
form, while women used the long-handled type
known as *e-kagami*. The thick-braided, elaborately tasseled red silken cord threaded through a protrusion in
the center of the mirror's back is proportionately
heavy in appearance, projecting a masculine elegance.
The back of the mirror is embellished with a serpen-
tine form shown weaving in and out of clouds, suggesting the appearance of a "rain dragon."

The background to the hydrangea inlay consists of
five leaves growing from a central stem. The gracefully curved lacquer painting of the stem and two of the
leaves are executed in the *fundame* technique, in which
gold powders too fine to polish are sprinkled on the
surface, creating a matte finish. The remaining three
leaves consist of inlays, one of pottery with a green
glaze, another of red lacquer (*tsuishu*), and the third of
a gray metal, probably a lead alloy. The metal has oxidized to a grainy white finish because its surface was
not lacquered, an effect the artist probably foresaw.

The veins of the leaves have been incised for
definition.

Each petal of the hydrangea cluster is a carefully
carved and polished inlay of mother-of-pearl with
softly rounded edges that slope up for definition, giving shape and mass to the cluster of florets, which
comprise a single huge blossom.

The cloth is of gold *taka maki-e*, with its undersurface represented by a finish of sprinkled silver powders
applied in a manner that simulates the shadow and
texture of the undulating material. The metal of the
mirror, executed in black-lacquered *sabi urushi*, has been
carefully molded, incised, polished, and finished to
resemble the dark metal alloy known as *shakudō*. The
effect is darker than is usually seen in mirrors of this
type, but suggests a somber and serious tone harmo-
nious with the overall composition. The silk cords
and tassels are of red lacquer. The braiding and texture
of the tassels has been expertly replicated.

The interior compartment has been fitted with a
water dropper and inkstone, set in a sprinkled gold
ground that is not of the same period as the lid. The
box is larger than most of this type, which suggests it
may have been made as a special order .

CONNOISSEURSHIP: The piece of fabric flows over the
edge and onto the side of the lid. This elegant, subtle
gesture calls attention to the edging surrounding the
surface panel of the lid. Although the box is unsigned,
its style suggests that its maker was Mochizuki
Hanzan (active in the mid-eighteenth century), a follower of Ogawa Haritsu. It has been assumed that the
two artists, if they met at all, had contact with each
other in Edo when Haritsu was an old man and
Hanzan quite young. Hanzan greatly admired the
master's style and often copied it. This composition
also shows Hon'ami Kōetsu's influence in its use of
broad, massive inlays.

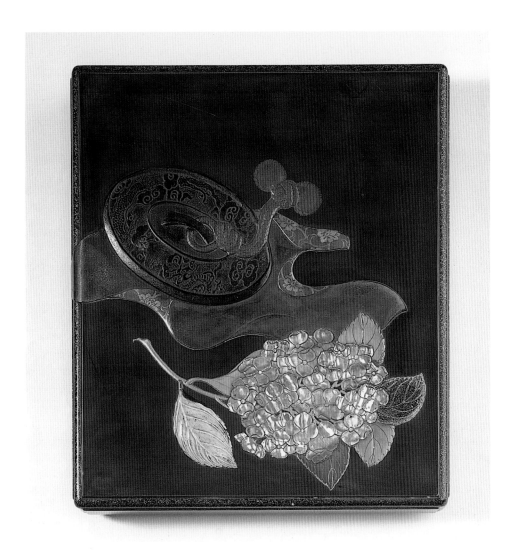

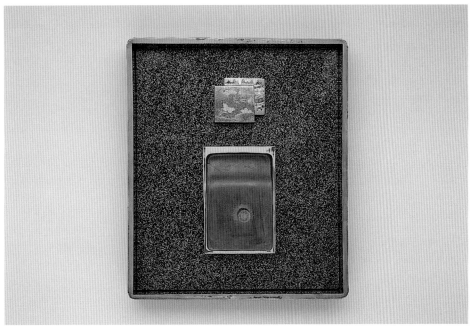

Above: exterior of the lid. Below: interior of the box.

27

Inkstone box (suzuribako)

An open boat amid reeds, tied to a piling on which an egret perches.

Edo period, 18th century.
Dimension: L 8 ½ in x W 8 ½ in x H 1 ¾ in
(21.6 x 21.6 x 4.5 cm)

This scene was first displayed on an inkstone box in the sixteenth century by Hon'ami Kōetsu, whose original set the pattern for subsequent interpretations.[32] It alludes to a chapter in *The Tale of Genji* in which Prince Genji takes the Lady Ukifune in a boat across the Uji river in midwinter. The starkness of the season and her state of mind are reflected in the empty boat among the sparse reeds. The lone egret reinforces the poignant solitude of the scene.

The stark black ground of night is broken only by the slight scattering of gold flakes in *hirame*, sprinkled between alternating layers of *nashiji urushi*. This type of clear orange-toned lacquer lends a tinted cast to some of the particles, imparting a sense of space.

The boat is made of lead-covered *sabi urushi* coated with a thin layer of black lacquer, then rubbed away in certain places. The darkened tone contrasts dramatically with the interior of the boat and the overhanging reeds, which are of plain gold *fundame*.

The egret, executed in white ceramic inlay with a crackled glaze, sits on the cross section of the piling, which is of the same material as the boat. The reeds have been dramatized with inlay of mother-of-pearl and sprinkled gold.

The inside of the lid is decorated with a "wind screen," a wide, single-paneled device used in winter to block drafts in the long halls of an aristocrat's house. The seven flowers and grasses of autumn gracefully decorate its surface. The screen's outer supports, usually made of wood, are represented here in dull silver,

and its depiction is enhanced by a red lacquer edging surrounding the central panel.

Inset in the lower left corner of the screen is a tiny inlay of white ceramic inscribed with red underglaze characters. The seal reads "Kan," which is a sobriquet of Ogawa Haritsu; however, when presented in a white cartouche, as here, it usually refers to Haritsu's follower, Mochizuki Hanzan. Adjacent to the screen is a vase containing the same flowers that decorate the brush tray next to the inkstone. A water dropper shaped like a crescent moon completes the set.

CONNOISSEURSHIP: The general theme of this box is loneliness and the melancholy of autumn, as represented on both the exterior and interior of the lid. The artist's original intent is most apparent in the spiral of the rope mooring the boat to the piling, the beauty of the inlays, and the delicate workmanship of the wind screen.

Unfortunately, the interior of this box has been embellished at a later date. The vase of flowers, positioned too close to the wind screen on the interior of the lid, was added recently. It closely resembles the floral cluster on the brush tray, which may also be a recent addition. In any event, the two floral sections (except for the inlay forming the long-necked vase) differ from the rest of the box in subject matter, color, style, and the lacquer techniques employed. These additions detract from the stark quality of loneliness expressed in the composition on the inside of the lid.

Top: exterior of the lid. Left: detail of the lid. Above right: interiors of the box and lid. Below right: detail of inside of the lid, showing the ceramic inlay.

28
Inkstone box (suzuribako)

Cherry blossoms hanging over a woven fence.

Edo period, 17th century.
Dimensions: L 9 in x w 8 ½ in x H 1 ⅞ in
(22.9 x 21.6 x 4.8 cm)

A smooth basketweave fence with a herringbone pattern of rectangles occupies the lower three-quarters of the lid, pushing the floral design into the upper quarter. The use of such an elevated horizon is a typical Japanese compositional device. The two vertical metallic inlays representing the fence's support posts break up the repetitive design, while directing the eye upward to the dense clusters of cherry blossoms made with appliqués of silver foil. One suddenly notices the small patches of plain, subtly exposed *nashiji* that have been interspersed to contrast with the gray, oxidized silver petals.

No motif is more important in Japanese art and literature than the double-petaled cherry blossoms that erupt but briefly, in early spring. For centuries Japanese poets have dwelt on their fragility and fleeting span of life. The beauty of women was compared to that of the cherry blossom, which, because of its short life (about five days) came to symbolize the transience of life. For the samurai, whose greatest fear was to suffer the indignities of old age, it represented the desire to die in a blaze of energy (hopefully in battle) at the height of his youth and beauty.

A tenth-century poem by an unknown poet summarizes this philosophy:

Nokori naku	It is just because
Chiru zo medetaki	They scatter without a trace
Sakurabana	That cherry blossoms
Arite yo no naka	Delight us so, for in this world
Hate no ukereba	Lingering means ugliness[33]

Care must be taken to differentiate the shape of the cherry blossom from that of the plum (see entry 1). The former is always notched in the middle of each petal, while the latter is simply curved.

The demimonde of the Yoshiwara celebrated the coming of spring by presenting its new stars to the public. Dressed in formal regalia and accompanied by their full entourage, the courtesans paraded through the main street either singly or in groups. The bold floral patterns on their costumes often featured cherry blossoms, so rich in associations.

The interior of the box displays two scenes that are associated with *meisho*, or "famous places." The waterwheel on the underside of the lid alludes to a bridge over the Uji River southeast of Kyoto, a image already famous by the sixteenth century.[34]

This type of waterwheel raises water from a river for use in irrigation channels. Here, the cups that scoop up the water are inlays of sliced lead, attached to a circular rim supported by spokes radiating from the center hub. The metal axle, resting on a notched branch anchored in the riverbank, is made of silver *taka maki-e*. The hub of the wheel is in gold leaf, while the spokes are rendered in gold *hira maki-e*. The ebb and flow of the water lapping against the riverbank has been painstakingly finished in gold *fundame*.

A second famous place is alluded to inside the bottom section of the box. The water dropper and inkstone occupy their appropriate places on the left. Adjacent to them is a fitted rectangular tray for writing brushes and other implements. It is decorated with jutting rocks and a high waterfall, a reference to the Nunobiki Falls on the Ikuta River in Kobe. The beginning of spring is suggested by a blossoming plum tree depicted in a frontal two-dimensional presentation typical of the period. Both the falls and flowers are of silver, and the contours of the rocks are further heightened by the addition of tiny squares cut from the same metal (*kimetsuke*).

CONNOISSEURSHIP: The original components of a set are often lost. Here a multicolored cloisonné water dropper has been exchanged for the original (note the darkened contour still visible as a border around the substitute). It is obviously the wrong color, style,

Interiors of the box and the lid.

shape, and material for this box, and its brightly colored pattern clashes with the subdued quadrant of buds and flowers that surrounds it. The inkstone is also a replacement, as it appears too new and its corners are too sharp to date from this period. Because inkstones often broke and water droppers were lost, the cutouts made in the insert to hold such accoutrements were often resized, as in this example. The appliqués seen on this box were made by rolling the silver alloy[35] on a surface and then cutting the desired outline with a tool resembling a cookie cutter, which accounts for the uniformity in size noted here.

29
Inkstone box (suzuribako)

Decorated with an eight-paneled screen.

Edo period, late 17th to early 18th century.
Dimensions: L 8 ¾ in x W 8 ⅛ in x H 1 ⅝ in
(22.2 X 20.7 X 4.1 cm)

As stated previously (see entry 17), boxes made with inverted corners (*irizumi*) are usually of excellent quality. The applied-gold ground that acts as the backdrop for the elegant screen depicted on the cover of this box is in *hirame-ji:* tiny circular flakes of flattened pure gold were placed discretely on the black lacquer ground. Care was taken not to let the particles overlap so that the contrast would be sharper.

The cornering of the lid where the four sides are joined to the central panel was formed with an extra ridge of dark gold that sets this area apart from the panels. This surface has been decorated with a floral scroll pattern that serves to demonstrate the special care that was given to the overall design.

The screen is shown open, as though being viewed, and its end panel is doubled back to expose the geometric fret pattern of its quilted back. The front panels of the screen are decorated with the seven flowers and grasses of autumn, rendered in the soft, smoothly flowing *yamato-e style.* Different shapes of *kirigane* (cut gold) have been applied in some areas to provide highlights contrasting with the matte finish typical of *fundame.* The edges of the eight panels and their mounts have been reinforced by what appears to be a metal brace, but is actually made of lacquer, with its outer edges highlighted in gold *hira maki-e.*

The bottom part of the box is divided into two almost equal sections. On the left is a softly curved inkstone with sprinkled gold edges. The metal water dropper above it is in the form of two interlocking chrysanthemums, echoing the theme of autumn on the screen. One blossom is in gold and the other in the fox-red finish known as *akagane.* The right section of the base, which holds the fitted tray for brushes and writing implements, is decorated with a delicate rendition of a small mound of rocks in gold and silver *taka maki-e.* In contrast to all the gold, three herons have been rendered in pure sprinkled silver (*gimpun*) with slight gold highlights.

On the underside of the lid, this scene continues, expanding into a landscape. A small fishing village nestles in a rocky promontory, with the rocks, trees, and houses rendered in the various techniques of *hira maki-e* and *taka maki-e.* Some distance away, a lone Chinese-style pavilion is situated near the water's edge. Smooth gold areas in *togidashi* are graded out from the shoreline to suggest low tide and shadows in the shallows.

The ground is in the same fine *hirame* particles seen on the lid, but here they have been applied sparingly to allow the black of night to show through. Such work invites the mind to rest or wander imaginatively, perhaps in preparation for creating a poem or a painting, thus fulfilling the purpose of this box. Lead alloy has been applied to protect the edges of the box.

CONNOISSEURSHIP: This is one of the finest boxes in the collection. The most notable feature is the interior, where a complete and continuous composition becomes apparent when the inside of the lid and the bottom section are placed side by side. Although most inkstone containers repeat themes from surface to surface, few are as detailed and finely finished as this. Its modest but poetic design, executed only in gold and silver powders, demonstrates exceptional workmanship.

Above: exterior of the lid. Below: interiors of the box and lid.

30

Inkstone box (suzuribako)

An open fan decorated with a monkey perched on a persimmon tree.

Edo period, early 18th century.
Dimensions: L 9 in x w 8 ⅜ in x H 1 ¾ in
(22.9 x 21.3 x 4.5 cm)

The only species of monkey native to Japan has brownish-yellow fur, a short tail, and a bright red face. In Japanese folklore these monkeys are usually associated with persimmons, a fruit they seem to enjoy. These animals are much loved in Japan and are thought of as messengers for such Shinto deities as Kōshin, god of the roads. Temples are devoted to them, and they are one of the twelve animal signs of Japan's Chinese-style astrological system.

Flat, stiff fans (*uchiwa*) were originally introduced to Japan from China, but the folding fan (*ōgi*) was invented by the Japanese, possibly in the ninth century. The folding fan shown on this inkstone box has ten ribs, but the number of ribs of a folding fan can range from three to thirty-eight, depending on its purpose.

This box, which combines elaborate design and ornate embellishment, offers the viewer a unique opportunity to study techniques now obsolete. Paramount is the use of the technique known as *hirame*, which may be seen on the rich ground of the lid's surface. Here, irregularly shaped tiny particles of flattened gold (*hirame*) are laid in individually so that they are set off by the black of the underlacquering.

The form of the open fan superimposed on the top of the lid was first contoured in thick *sabi urushi* to produce a deep three-dimensional effect. Surface treatment with gold would be applied to this area only after it was completely dry, its shape approved by the artist, and it had received a final polish. At this point the ribs radiating from the central rivet were also delineated.

The landscape surrounding the monkey seated on the persimmon tree with its jutting branches includes a distant stream with moving water and a rocky promontory. Here again, black lacquer supplies the background color for the heavy decoration to follow.

A large mass of irregular flakes of pure gold, larger in size than the previously noted *hirame* and sometimes referred to as Gyōbu *hirame* (after Gyōbu Tarō, the mid-Edo-period artist who invented the technique), acts as a backdrop for the monkey and part of the tree. The flakes have been carefully and individually placed side by side, as was customary in this now-obsolete technique. It has been postulated that these flakes have irregular edges because they were individually handmade—a time-consuming process that may have been reason enough for the abandonment of the technique.

The dominant figure of the monkey is formed of some underlying thickening agent to which various gold techniques have been applied. Its face, of inlaid carved coral, simulates the facial color of the real animal. *Hira maki-e*, *taka maki-e*, and *sabi urushi* covered with sprinkled gold powder have been added to complete the scene.

Especially fascinating is the way the artist depicted the shadows between the folds of the fan. By allowing more of the black underlacquer to show through on one side of each fold (working from the center out), he created alternating dim and light bands that simulate shadows. Clouds at the upper edge of the fan convey a dreamlike quality. The struts are made of metal inlays in alternating *shibuichi* (a copper and silver alloy) and brass.

While the extravagant, flamboyant top of the lid depicts images of daytime, the interior of the box is its opposite in mood and content: the quiet of night and the serenity of a slowly moving stream lined with clusters of chrysanthemums.

On the left side of the bottom of the box, passing underneath the inkstone and below the water dropper, are subtle lines that suggest the side of a mountain. The rimmed tray to the right of the inkstone features sprigs of pampas grasses and a cluster of chrysanthemums. Each flower and leaf, framed by a darkened ground of sprinkled gold on lacquer, has been toned orange by the addition of gamboge.

The underside of the lid expands this landscape with a background of sprinkled gold powders on deep-toned lacquer. Peeking out of a cloudy sky, a

Interiors of the box and lid.

silver three-quarter moon shines down on a silent current of water that brushes by the shores. A carefully delineated, lush profusion of chrysanthemums and pampas grasses signifies the height of the poignant autumn season. In the distance are two fishing weirs, in delicate *hira maki-e*. Different shapes of cut gold foil (*kirigane*) are blended into the cloud formation. All edges of the box and its interior tray are lined with a lead alloy to protect them from chipping.

CONNOISSEURSHIP: In its combination of flamboyance and subtlety, its utilization of the finest unadulterated materials, and the precision of its techniques and execution, this box represents the acme of lacquerware in the first half of the eighteenth century. All surfaces have been given a ground of colored lacquer on which gold has been sprinkled or placed, a technique that differs completely from *nashiji*, in which the gold may be adulterated and then curled for better effect.

31
Inkstone box (suzuribako)

Two birds in flight over a shoreline are outlined against the night sky.

Edo period, 18th century.
Dimensions: L 6 ⅞ in x w 7 ⅛ in x H 1 ¼ in
(17.5 x 18.1 x 3.2 cm)

T his box is a good example of how art can document history. Depicted is a now lost picturesque element of the Japanese countryside: a *jakago* or gabion, a basketlike structure usually woven of wood strips and filled with stones, typically used to prevent soil erosion. In the twentieth century, reinforced concrete rendered it obsolete.

Almost two-thirds of the lid is occupied by a black night sky, which serves as a striking background for colorful ceramic inlays in the form of two night-flying cuckoos (*hototogisu*). Made of porcelain and then covered with colored glazes in the Edo style, these birds counterbalance the rest of the composition.

To form the rocks contained within the *jakago*, a large mass of *sabi urushi* was applied to the ground. Then various materials were inserted as inlays. Nuggets of coral, malachite, and tiny pebblelike forms finished in dull silver powder duplicate the natural coloring of stones enclosed in the net. The woven slats that simulate the appearance of webbing are rectangular pieces of mother-of-pearl.

Two other inlays simulate a cross brace, the joint of which is bound together with a lacquer rope finished in gold powder. The front brace is made of bone refinished in brown *urushi*, while the back one is coated in a metallic-colored lacquer.

The inside of the box contains an inkstone set in the center of the base. The gourd-shaped copper water dropper fits snugly into its separate thin crimped-edge silver surround. This in turn is set within a brass fitting shaped as a spray of leaves. The whole fixture does not conform to the cutout in the lacquer base in which it sits. Its jagged contour is too loose. Close examination reveals it to be a later replacement.

Two landscapes in overlapping fan-shaped reserves decorate the inside of the lid. A bare, leafless willow tree in the scene on the right suggests winter. The land area is executed in pale silver and gold *taka maki-e* reserve. The design of plantains and flowing water on the other fan-shaped reserve symbolizes summer.

The presence of two fans and the placement of one over the other suggests that this box was made as a commemorative piece for two lovers, a theme first introduced on the lid. The cuckoos emphasize the reference to summer. Perhaps the happy lovers met in the summer and parted in winter. If so, the lonely willow makes a poetic allusion to the sadness of separation.

CONNOISSEURSHIP: The literature of the Edo period reflects the values of the newly emerging middle-class culture. New forms of theater such as Kabuki and the puppet drama Bunraku developed for the common people. Stories of unrequited or forbidden love were most popular. The bondage of women during the Edo period was the most complete in all of Japanese history. Marriage in this Neo-Confucian society was strictly for the continuance of the family, and women were considered chattels to be used to build family alliances and to bear children. A woman's loyalty was first to her father, then to her husband, and after that, to her son. Extramarital affairs often led to the woman's suicide; in rare instances the man might join her. Wealthy merchants might occasionally marry a *geisha* or courtesan with whom they had fallen in love by buying her contract from the house employing her, but that was the exception, not the rule. It is not surprising, then, that many lacquer boxes of the Edo period are decorated with hidden symbols—allusions to events in a secret affair that only the owner would understand (see also entry 26).

Above: exterior of the lid. Below: interiors of the box and lid.

32
Mirror box (kagamibako)

Decorated with two fans.

Edo period, 18th century.
Dimensions: DIA 4 in X H 1 in
(10.2 X 2.5 cm)

I n this mirror box, poetic overtones are achieved by varying the size of the gold particles added to lacquer of uniform color using a variety of techniques. The three-quarter-opened fan on the right, decorated with a few sprigs of pampas grass and the wild flowering grass known as *fujibakama* (agueweed) in pale *fundame* and *hira maki-e*, indicate autumn. The fully opened fan behind it and to the left is decorated with chrysanthemums beside a flowing stream and dewdrops in the air.

The scenes allude to an old Chinese legend that relates the story of a Chinese youth—known in Japan as Kiku Jidō, or the Chrysanthemum Youth—who was the favorite of the emperor. He was exiled as a result of a breach of etiquette, but before he departed his beloved emperor taught him a sacred verse that would keep him safe for a long time. After arriving in a distant place where chrysanthemums flourished, he passed the time and kept the magical phrase in his memory by inscribing it on the petals of chrysanthemums. He would then cast the dew-laden flowers into a nearby stream, from which he also drank.

In the Japanese Noh play *Kiku Jidō*, which is based on this legend, the young man suddenly realizes that he is no longer beset by such earthly problems as aging and ill health. After making the connection between his failure to age and his drinking of the water into which dew from the inscribed flowers has fallen, he returns home with this magical potion and gives it to his cherished emperor. At the chrysanthemum festival on the ninth day of the ninth month, according to the old lunar calendar, wine is consumed in remembrance of this legend. Perhaps the participants hope that it contains some degree of truth.

The lid of the mirror box is covered with a *nashiji* ground, on which notched, five-petaled cherry blossoms, representing spring and youthful beauty, are well defined in raised gold.

CONNOISSEURSHIP: Typically the design found on a lacquer box reflects a specific purpose. Here a smaller, three-quarter-opened fan is set against a larger fully opened one, suggesting a couple. Hence the box was probably a memento of a special occasion they wanted to commemorate.

33
Medicine container (inrō)

Decorated with designs in the form of two sword guards. The usual side channels are absent.

Momoyama period, late 16th or early 17th century.
Dimensions: H 4 ¼ in x w 3 ½ in
(11.4 x 8.9 cm)

By the seventeenth century it was customary for men to wear a portable, multitiered container called an *inrō* suspended from the *obi*, or sash, used to fasten the kimono. The literal meaning of the word *inrō* is "seal basket," and they are thought to have originally been used to carry one's identity seal and ink. Eventually, however, the *inrō's* principal use became transporting medicines in powder or pellet form, kept dry by the tightly sealed compartments.

Historians have various theories as to the *inrō's* origin and shape. These include speculation as to a fifteenth-century Chinese origin, as well as conjecture that their shape is derived from the large, tiered Japanese boxes used to store medicines on shelves. There may be some truth to both of these ideas.

Style, shape, design, and technique help date *inrō*. The earliest examples, used by the samurai, had plain black grounds.[36] At that time artisans still flaked their own gold, which lent a deep, rich luster to the decoration. As demand increased, however, specialists began making gold flakes in a uniform set of sizes. The addition of the orange coloring agent gamboge to the base and covering coats enabled artisans to simulate the appearance of more expensive, purer materials. Eventually, all the techniques available for lacquer boxes were incorporated into the production of *inrō*. Although *inrō* were made of lacquer, the majority of the great artists who created boxes for the elite rarely decorated *inrō*. Instead, this genre developed its own artists, who in turn rarely worked on boxes. By the second half of the seventeenth century, *inrō* artists began to sign their work.

The eighteenth century saw the mature development of *inrō*. Their exteriors provided a ground for remarkably creative expression; often both sides were used for a single continuous composition. The discriminating and the rich wore an *inrō* at all times. *Inrō* were featured in the luxurious type of woodblock prints called *surimono*, and Kabuki actors were occasionally portrayed with elegant examples hanging from their sashes.

This unusual *inrō* is an early transitional piece. Although it has three sections plus a cover, it does not have the typical side channels necessary for suspension from the sash (see entry 34). In fact, its straight bottom suggests that it was meant to rest on a flat surface. However, it is also small enough to have been carried, either in the breast fold of a kimono or within the sleeve and may have served as either a stationary or portable container.

The designs on the sides and top of this container were executed at different times. The larger of the two, which flows over the top of the lid and down one side, is in the shape of an early-seventeenth-century sword guard (*tsuba*) in the openwork style known as *sukashi*. Cleaning the spaces between the tendrils that embellish its curved rain-dragon design has revealed the original mother-of-pearl background. Close examination confirms that this was completed at the same time as the surface ground of the body of the container, which was executed in a *sabi urushi* gold finish technique.

The other *tsuba* design, which shows the Zen patriarch Bodhidharma (called Daruma in Japanese), was probably added at a later date, as its subject matter, shape, composition, and techniques are more common to late-eighteenth-century lacquers.

CONNOISSEURSHIP: The original square design on the speckled mother-of-pearl ground was large enough to decorate the *inrō* adequately. *Sukashi*-style *tsuba* stopped being used by the end of the seventeenth century, when the fashion in sword guards changed. The *tsuba* adorned with a portrait of Bodhidharma is executed in colored lacquer simulating the alloy known as *shakudō*, a technique not common in lacquerwork until the late eighteenth century. The dating of this object is thus based in part on when certain styles of sword guards became popular—but even more telling is the evidence provided by the laquerwork itself, and knowledge of the periods in which specific techniques prevailed.

Front and back panels of the inrō.

34
Medicine container (inrō)

The front panel depicts Raiden, Shinto god of thunder and lightning, against an unusual *zonsei nuri* background.

Edo period, 18th century.
Dimensions: H 2 ⅝ in x W 2 ¾ in
(6.7 x 6.9 cm)

Traditional accounts of the origin of the custom of wearing *inrō* trace it to the early-seventeenth-century female dancer known as Okuni, who is also regarded as the originator of the Kabuki drama. Audiences at her performances noticed the decorative and colorful paraphernalia hanging from her belt, which can be seen on screens, painted at the time, that depict these occasions. Among the many articles that can be seen, secured by a *netsuke*, or toggle, was the multitiered, beautifully lacquered medicine carrier known as an *inrō*.[37]

Inrō were both costly and time-consuming to make. The wooden inner core, which was created by specialists, required aging for at least ten years, and the outer surfaces were customarily embellished with *maki-e*, which typically used gold.

Inrō were not affected by the sumptuary laws of the period, and wearing them became popular as an indication of the owner's wealth. At the same time, the tightly constructed, compartmentalized box served as a perfect repository for the patented medicines and natural herbs so enjoyed by the Japanese.[38] The airtight compartments kept the tiny pellets and powders, wrapped in paper, fresh and dry despite Japan's constant humidity.

From early-seventeenth-century screens and paintings which show only the front of the *inrō*, it is clear that the themes presented were executed in fairly simple designs and techniques. Such subjects as leaves, grasses, or even a picture of a horse were applied to a basic black ground. These early *inrō* were always shown accompanied by a leather money pouch (*kinchaku*).[39] Both objects were strung separately, attached to a single *netsuke*, and hung from the sash on the right side, toward the back of the body. Then the fashion changed, probably because the money pouch was so vulnerable to theft, and, by the middle of the seventeenth century, it had disappeared from view. The *inrō* now appeared alone, more elaborate and with a bow at its base.

The ensemble was put together in the following manner. Colored silk cord was first fashioned into a double or triple bow, with the loops locked as part of the knotting process. The bow was then centered at the bottom of the *inrō*, and the cord's two ends were strung up and through its side channels and passed through a decorative lock-bead, or *ojime* (see entry 55). The ends were tightly secured after having been passed through the appropriate openings in a *netsuke*, which was used as a toggle to keep the cord from slipping from behind the sash where it was anchored. The whole ensembles was often given a unified theme. Unfortunately the original components of most ensembles have become lost or separated.

Zonsei nuri, the type of decoration used in the present example, was, according to some sources, devised by a Chinese lacquerer named Cun Xing (Zonsei in Japanese), whose work displayed red, green, and yellow lacquer on a black ground.[40] It is often confused with the irregular mottled patterning seen in *wakasa nuri* (see entry 55).

Gold particles incorporated into the black ground of this *inrō*, combined with yellow and red lacquers, give it an overall ocher tone. Although the metal inlays depicting the lightning bolts are muted, they can be seen clearly because their shape is so different from the curves of the ground.

The amusing and determined god of thunder, fashioned in the pure *maki-e* technique of *togidashi*, appears suspended in action, as the wind blows his hair and makes his long scarves trail behind. This demonlike creature hurls lightning bolts with one hand and creates thunder by rattling the drum in his other. Drums also encircle his body in a large orb.

CONNOISSEURSHIP: *Maki-e* is added to a complicated ground such as this only after the work is finished and has been completely sealed.

Front and back panels of the inrō.

35
Long scroll box (nagafubako)

Decorated with a crest of five ginkgo leaves in a circular pattern.

Muromachi period, late 15th or early 16th century.
Dimensions: L 15 ¼ in x W 3 ⅝ in x H 3 ⅛ in
(38.7 x 9.2 x 7.9 cm)

Covered boxes used for storage or transport of scrolls, called *fubako*, were produced in two main formats. This piece is an example of the *nagafubako*, or long scroll box, more likely to have been used to hold pictorial scrolls, such as a treasured painting, rather than letters or documents. The deep overlapping lid on this type of box kept dust and other contaminants from affecting the contents, and the cords usually attached to the sides kept the contents from shifting when handled. Often the wood or ivory knobs attached to the scroll were fitted securely into notches cut in wooden wedges inserted at both ends of the box's interior. The shape of this type of box probably originated from that of early sutra containers, which had a shallower lid.

The example shown here is decorated with the pattern of a *mon*, or family crest, a motif that has a long and distinguished history in the evolution of Japanese design. By the end of the Nara period (645–794), fabrics used in Japanese court costumes reflected current Chinese fashion in the use of repeat patterns known as *yūsoku mon'yō*, consisting of individual ideographs inconspicuously interwoven into the fabric.[41] These became the basis for the formation of heraldic emblems on lacquers during the Heian period (794–1185). As might be expected, social status was a key factor in establishing the widespread use of these family crests. Most of the ruling elite were related, and crests helped to identify where one stood in this complex web of kinship and to distinguish Kyoto court aristocrats from their less important provincial cousins. During festivals and other social events, family crests emblazoned on the ox carts used as transport by aristocrats were an aid in determining who were the closest relatives of the imperial family and the powerful Fujiwara regents. Those of the highest status were allowed to park closest to the imperial gates.[42] The style and subject matter of these designs also reflected the Heian elite's preoccupation with poetry. Most popular at the time were circular medallions based on natural forms, especially grasses and foliage. These same themes dominated heraldic designs throughout the following Kamakura period (1185–1392), when, with the emergence of the military class, family crests came into even more general use, and appeared on all possessions of a samurai's family.

The *mon* on this box is formed from five ginkgo leaves arranged in a circle (although it has also been suggested that this pattern may represent that of the *nadeshiko*, or fringed pink). The ginkgo tree originated in China. Perhaps because of its longevity, as well as its ability to survive extremes in temperature, the tree acquired an almost religious aura, and ginkgo trees were planted near Shinto shrines and within the grounds of Buddhist temples.

The working of the box is a fine example of the early and difficult technique known as *hyōmon*, in which thin-sliced silver and gold foil are cut into a pattern and then glued over a finished ground, here executed in *nashiji*.

Although a few of the metallic leaves appear to be replacements, most are of the original period. The exfoliation displayed here is a result of wear or possibly the absence of a coat of lacquer thick enough to keep the underlying glue from deteriorating. In the early technique of *heidatsu* the finishing coat of lacquer was deliberately scraped away to reveal the shine of the pure metal. This technique, however, fell into disuse before this piece was made.

The leaf and bud patterns that unfurl from either side of the ginkgo clusters are similar to those found in the writing boxes in the Tokyo National Museum decorated with plum or chrysanthemum blossoms.[43] This leaf-scroll pattern evolved into the conventional scrollwork termed *karakusa* (literally, "Chinese foliage"). The slightly raised surfaces (in *hira maki-e*) are made of gold *fundame*, in which fine gold powder is sprinkled on so abundantly that the area it fills looks like solid gold. Due to the fineness of the particles used for this effect, the surface cannot be polished, and therefore *fundame* always appears as a dull or matte finish.

Above: overview of the box. Below: detail of one side of the box.

The interior of this box is decorated with the same fine *nashiji* finish as its exterior. The matching metal ring attachments on both sides of the bottom are for silk cords that were tied to secure the lid. The trilobed cutaway on the bottom edge of the lid is typical of this style of container. Its purpose was to allow the metal rings below to move up and down without damaging the fragile lacquer finish of the lid.

CONNOISSEURSHIP: Although parts of the pure gold leaf on a few of the leaves have been replaced, and particles of the slivered silver are missing, this is indeed a very early and excellent example of Muromachi lacquer.

Detail of the lid of the box.

36
Circular incense container (kōgō)

Covered with a stylized design of paulownia.

Momoyama period, 16th century.
Dimensions: DIA 3 in x H 1 ¼ in
(7.6 x 3.2 cm)

Since ancient times the Japanese aristocracy, following the lead of the Chinese, has had a high regard for the paulownia, or *kiri*. According to Chinese legends it was the only tree upon which the sacred phoenix would rest. Its tiny bell-shaped flowers produce seeds used in the moon cakes that the Chinese traditionally ate during the autumn festival in the eighth month of the old lunar calendar.

In medieval Japan the paulownia and the chrysanthemum became established as crests of the imperial family. During the Muromachi period the newly ascendant Ashikaga shoguns were allowed to use the paulownia symbol. Later military rulers such as Oda Nobunaga (1534–82) and Toyotomi Hideyoshi (1536–98) also used it, thus implying a direct connection to the imperial house.

Hideyoshi used it in the "five-seven" combination of blossoms (see entry 39) on all of his possessions, and variations of it on objects he sent abroad as gifts of state. The inclusion of the paulownia motif on all the lacquers donated to the temple Kōdaiji by his widow helped to make it a popular symbol (see entry 12). Following Hideyoshi's death, the Tokugawa shōguns, in a declaration of independence, adopted the *aoi* (hollyhock) crest as their family emblem.

The pattern displayed on this box also appears on several early objects, one of them a covered chest (*karabitsu*) owned by the Hōkoku Shrine in Kyoto.[44] Described by scholars as "paulownia scrolls,"[45] this pattern is also featured on other works of the late sixteenth and early seventeenth centuries.

The designs on this box are in gold *hira maki-e* on a *nashiji* ground. Its interior is embellished with sparse *nashiji* on a black ground, while the interior of the lid is also decorated with a pattern of a single paulownia cluster, surrounded by leaf scrollwork, in the *fundame* technique. The rims of the box are fortified in a lead alloy.

CONNOISSEURSHIP: This variation of the paulownia design was used especially on lacquers in the Kōdaiji style.

Above: exterior of the lid. Below: interior of the lid.

37
Incense burner (kōro)

Fitted with a perforated metal cover.

Edo period, late 17th or early 18th century.
Dimensions: D 3 ¾ in x H 2 ⅞ in
(9.5 x 7.3 cm)

Incense burners were common in most eighteenth-century Japanese homes. They often took the form of a simple dish in which a stick of incense was burned before a shrine as a symbol of respect and as an aid to meditation. In homes of great wealth, large grate-covered burners encased in wood were used to lend the clothing draped over them a clinging, sweet-smelling aroma. In earlier times, samurai would scent their helmets before battle in this fashion, as they thought the fragrance would help clear their minds.

Yabunouchi Chikushin (1678–1745), the great master of the Yabunouchi style of the tea ceremony, once wrote, "Incense is used in the tearoom ... to welcome the guest; to purify the spirit of the room; to show reverence when a scroll of painting or calligraphy is hung; when one guest has come early, to welcome the later guests; to cheer the dark of night; to warm an evening of snow or rain; to mark the events of the season."[46]

Most incense burners have the same *akoda* (melon or pumpkin) shape as the one shown here, and they were found in the boudoir, where they were often part of a lady's toilet ensemble, as well as in the tea house. (Incense was frequently burned while applying make-up.) In this particular example, the lacquer base is decorated with chrysanthemums and other flowers representing autumn, a theme often associated with the tea ceremony. Before the ceremony it was customary to perfume the room or the immediate area for the clarification of the mind and the relaxation of the body.

The lacquered part of the burner shown here is decorated with a ground of *nashiji*, after which images of several flowering grasses were applied in *hira maki-e fundame*. Three family crests (*mon*), two of which are identical, embellish the composition that circles the body of the container. The presence of two different crests signals that this was part of an aristocrat's wedding trousseau. The crest that appears only once shows two thin stalks of bamboo with five leaves within a circle. It is a variation on the crest of the Mōri family of Akao. The two identical designs, which are of crossed falcon feathers in a circle, represent the Abe family of Fukuyama.[47]

The cover is of pierced bronze in a basketweave pattern, and an extra edging of bronze has been added to protect the lacquered base.

CONNOISSEURSHIP: The careful match in the contours of the metal cover and liner of the burner are evidence of the quality of this object. The patina on these metal fittings is identical, further indication that the cover is original to the piece.

38
Group of three boxes
from an incense game

Decorated with two family crests.

Edo period, late 17th century.
Dimensions:
Square box: L 1 ¾ in x W 1 ¾ in x H 1 ½ in (4.5 x 4.5 x 3.8 cm)
Round box: DIA 1 ⅞ in x H 1 ¾ in (4.8 x 4.5 cm)
Round box: DIA 1 ¹⁵⁄₁₆ in. x H 2 ⅞ in (4.9 x 7.3 cm)

These three pieces are components of an incense game set (see entry 49 for a description of the game and its utensils). All are decorated with symbols of longevity (pine) and endurance (bamboo). The bamboo was esteemed as a symbol because it bent but did not break during the most terrible of storms.

The *mon*, or family crests, on either side of each of the boxes are both variations on older motifs. One crest has a five-notched-petal floral design of *nadeshiko*, or fringed pinks, in a cluster of three, not encircled. It represents the samurai family known as the Saitō. The crest on the obverse side combines a four-petaled flower with a curved motif based on the form of the old long sword, set in a circular surround. This is a variation on the crest awarded by the Tokugawa to the Matsuura family of Katsumoto in the early seventeenth century.

Of the three containers, the two rounded ones, lined with metal, were designed to hold the ash required for burning incense. The smaller of these is for burning the wood variety of incense and the deeper one for burning the tall, thin stick incense (*senkō*) seen in Buddhist temples. The other lidded container, a square-shaped box, has a deep, high-sided interior that probably held the mica chips on which the wood incense would be placed before burning.

All decoration is in *hira maki-e*, with veins and edging added in the *keuchi* technique and with *e-nashiji* as color contrast within the leaves.

CONNOISSEURSHIP: Completely intact incense sets are very rare. Components of a set were so attractive that family members used them for other purposes. Once separated, they were apt not to be reunited with the set, as was probably the case with these three boxes.

39
Tea whisk holder (chasenzutsu)

Decorated with a family crest on the lid.

Edo period, 17th or 18th century.
Dimensions: DIA 1 ⅝ in x H 3 ⅜ in
(4.1 x 8.6 cm)

The ceremonial tea whisk that was stored in this container was made of bamboo by an artisan who specialized in this craft. Such whisks are used in the tea ceremony to mix powdered green tea with hot water in a ceramic tea bowl.

The whisk is a unique item made from a section of the bamboo plant that has been specially selected by the craftsman. The segment that becomes the whisk is carefully cut, polished, slivered, soaked, and curled while still attached to the part that becomes the handle.

During the tea ceremony, the host or hostess briskly whisks the tea into a creamy froth with the split bamboo device. After a final shake, it is carefully placed upright at the side of the host or hostess. The whisk is used repeatedly in the same manner for every guest involved in the tea ceremony, and only after the entire ceremony is completed and the guests have departed is the whisk rinsed carefully and left to dry thoroughly before being put back into its container.

Each accoutrement of the tea ceremony, along with its individual covering cloth and outer storage box, is cherished by its owner, and the older an object becomes, the more it is revered. When a tea ceremony object becomes damaged, great effort is expended to restore it. The success of one such attempt may be observed in this lovely cylindrical container. The lacquered top of the lid is decorated with the "five-seven" paulownia-blossom design (*go-shichi no kirimon*) used as a family crest by the Toyotomi and a few other families. The design is in gold *fundame* on a black lacquer ground. Judging from the caramelization of the high-quality black ground and the detail of the work, it probably originated in the seventeenth century. Careful examination reveals that the lid may formerly have been attached to another object, and subsequently "married" to a new body.[48]

The container's outer surface is covered with square-cut pieces of mother-of-pearl painstakingly selected for color and size, and then carefully applied in a mosaic pattern on a black lacquer ground. The small gold appliqué on one side serves as an indicator to align the patterning on the top and bottom. This kind of thickly cut pale mother-of-pearl, however, is more characteristic of the eighteenth than the seventeenth century. Also, the shinier quality of the sprinkled gold used in the appliqué points to a later date than that of the lacquered upper surface. The interior and underside are finished in red lacquer.

CONNOISSEURSHIP: The gold powder used on the paulownia crest is darker in color and differs in texture from the gold in the appliqué on the side of the container. However, the most important factor in dating the piece is the presence of the appliqué. Seventeenth-century artists would have chosen subtler ways to indicate the alignment of the lid and bottom of the container, unless the owner's vision was impaired and he or she had requested the addition. An aristocrat would never have ordered such an obvious adornment, and an earlier artist would have used another, less obvious, approach.

40
Tea caddy (natsume)

Decorated with a "three-five" paulownia-blossom
crest (*san-go no kirimon*).

Edo period, 18th century.
Dimensions: DIA 2 ⅜ in x H 2 ⅜ in
(6.1 x 6.1 cm)

Tea caddies are classified by the type of tea they hold. The *chaire*, a ceramic container, usually with an ivory lid, is generally used to store *koicha*, or "thick" tea, while *usucha*, or "thin" tea, is customarily stored in a lacquer caddy known as a *natsume* (so named because its shape resembles that of the jujube fruit). The first *natsume* are said to have been created in the Momoyama period. Sen no Rikyū (1521–91), the creator of the formalized version of the tea ceremony that is still practiced today, preferred this shape.

Natsume come in three sizes: small, medium (the most common), and large. This one is medium-sized. In keeping with its simple contours, only two decorative formations break the high glossy shine of the finest quality *ro-iro*. On the lid is a paulownia crest in gold *fundame*, with the veins of the leaves left in reserve (*kakiwari*). The *san-go no kirimon* ("three-five" paulownia-blossom family crest), probably that of the Hosokawa family of Takase or Kumamoto, elegantly completes the stark, waxy black ground. The only

other design decorating the surfaces is a gold fret pattern in the shape of joined Buddhist crosses (*manji*), which appears as a horizontal band around the juncture of the lid and bottom sections.

CONNOISSEURSHIP: An important component of an accoutrement used in the tea ceremony is its form-fitting textile cover. This protects the surface of the object, and a knowledge of its pattern and stitching can also help in dating. The original outer box usually had an inscription on the cover attesting to the maker of the contents and sometimes the date. This form of documentary evidence was part of the heritage that accompanied most art objects in Japan, and it is especially important in the case of tea ceremony accoutrements. Unfortunately, until quite recently most people in the West did not understand the importance of the cloths that covered these kinds of objects, or the outer boxes that were originally used to store them. As a result, early and unknowledgeable Western collectors discarded them as a nuisance.

41
Tea utensil box (chabako)

Designed for travel, in the shape of two overlapping octagonal cylinders.

Edo period, late 17th or early 18th century.
Dimensions: L 6 ¾ in x w 3 ½ in x H 4 ⅛ in
(17.2 x 8.9 x 10.5 cm)

This finely decorated box was probably for the carrying of tea accoutrements while traveling. Its elegant shape and surface design undoubtedly reflect the taste of aristocratic owners.

Powdered tea suspended in hot water was first introduced as a beverage in China's Fukien province during the early Northern Song dynasty (960–1127). Its popularity was encouraged by the imperial court, which saw in tea an important source of tax revenue; however, the following prose-poem, thought to be the first inspired by tea, shows that it had more general appeal:

> The waters of Chien run true, cold, and pure.
> The tea people have already risen early,
> Facing the young shoots and spring rain,
> Plucking it, binding it, wrapped in spring ice.
> When it is pounded fine, a fragrant powder forms;
> Boiled freshly, a jade milk thickens.
> When you are feeling agitated, if you take one sip,
> How is it that you crave it like wine? [49]

The form of two interlocking octagons originated in China, the country from which tea came to Japan. Here these geometric shapes divide the top surface of this box into two design areas. Both sections are decorated with elegant depictions of *bonsai* trees of different types. On the left is a sharply truncated, ancient pine. The tree, and the earth and dish that hold it, are executed in gold *hira maki-e* and *taka maki-e*. A deep orange-toned lacquer (*nashiji*) defines the earth within the container, and tiny cut-gold squares (*kirigane*) pasted on the tree trunk provide contrast. Where the gold foil has been lost, the red lacquer undercoating that was used to lend the gold a rich, deep tone is exposed. The oval container that holds the *bonsai* is finished in piled gold, with a scrolling floral pattern decorating its concave lip.

The image on the right, in a subordinate position, is an equally aged plum tree with only a few blossoms and buds decorating its stark and otherwise empty branches. The petals made of silver powder give it added distinction. All the elements on this octagon have been finished in the same techniques and textures as its companion. Only the design on the lip of the dish differs, incorporating a twelve-petaled chrysanthemum motif in a repeat pattern.

Each octagon is set in a reserve of heavy gold, with tiny, delicate scroll work in *taka maki-e*, gold in one hexagon and silver in the other. A carefully matched border of diamond-shaped floral enclosures surrounds the upper and lower edges of the box and lid, respectively. Standing out against the intensely black, lacquered surfaces of each front and back panel in gold and silver *hira maki-e* is the *san-go no kirimon* ("three-five" paulownia-blossom family crest) of the Hosokawa family of Takase or Kumamoto.

The inside of the lid is decorated with a lacquer painting of protruding rocks. A long bridge with thick pilings extends from the shore over the water, and a double-roofed pavilion with a railing is shown at the far end of the bridge, where the tranquil night sky with its quarter moon may be enjoyed. The black lacquer ground with carefully graduated gold particles (*maki-bokashi*) suggests a sky filled with distant stars. The quarter moon is made of thick sprinkled silver covered with a lacquer coat to prevent oxidation.

The rocky formation on the left side of the composition follows the style of the Chinese-influenced Kanō school, which was heavily patronized by the Tokugawa shogunate.

CONNOISSEURSHIP: Although much has been written in English about the tea ceremony, little is available concerning the lacquer boxes associated with it. Much more research is necessary in this field.

Above: overview of the box. Below: interior of the lid.

42

Mirror box (kagamibako) and tiered incense container (jūkōgō)

The mirror box is inscribed on its inner surface with a poem celebrating the samurai spirit.

Edo period, early 18th century.
Dimensions: Mirror box: DIA 5 ¾ in x H 2 ½ in (14.6 x 6.4 cm)
Incense container: DIA 2 ¼ in x H 2 in (5.7 x 5.1 cm)

Although these two containers are of a later period, the artist has chosen the early style of frontal imagery that prevailed from the fifteenth to early seventeenth century.

Mirror box. The clematis, a flowering vine, grows from unseen roots at the bottom edge of the lower section of the box, and its leaves, buds, and blossoms emerge from the main stem as it spreads across the entire surface of the softly contoured lid. The overgrowth of the vine, which, despite its many offshoots, is a single plant, drops over the edges of the lid and continues along the circumference of the box.

The interior of the box also displays a clematis design, here encircling a matte gold rectangular plaque in the shape of a poetry slip, upon which a poem is written in the cursive script known as *sōsho*. The gist of the poem is that, despite the transience of human life, the loyalty of a samurai to his master will never change.[50] Since this poem appears on the inside lid of a mirror box, the lines may refer to the tradition of bequeathing a special object to one's master, thereby continuing loyal service even after death.

Once the mirror that is held within the box has been removed, a flaming *tama*, or sacred jewel, finished in *togidashi*, stands out against the pure sprinkled gold of the ground.

Incense container. This container is two-tiered, with a cover, and is octagonal in shape. The lid is contoured as an eight-petaled flower, and the clematis pattern on the lid and sides repeats that of the mirror box.

Examination of the interior reveals the construction of the box. A special type of incense was probably stored in layers in its tiers.

The lacquer techniques used in the finishing of both boxes are identical. The background is of *nashiji* with *taka maki-e* contoured flowers, the surfaces of which have been first underpainted in black lacquer. Sprinkled gold powders in the matte finish of *fundame* were applied to those areas that would become the vines, leaves, and parts of the flowers. Then certain parts of the leaves were scratched away (*harigaki*), revealing the black underpainting which became the veins. This technique must be executed very carefully so that the quill or other device used for the purpose does not penetrate beyond the thin layer of black. The detailing was done through the use of *keuchi*, that is, the addition of an edging in gold *hira maki-e*. The poem was written in *hira maki-e* against a *fundame*-finished plaque applied to the *nashiji* ground.

CONNOISSEURSHIP: Customarily, mirror boxes and tiered boxes were part of a woman's trousseau; however, in this case one must wonder. The poem is obviously designed to appeal to a man, and it is known that men also used mirrors to help them dress their elaborate hairstyles. Although these boxes are not decorated with a formal family crest, their apparent age, the approach to the design accompanied by superb workmanship, and the inclusion of the type of poem evident on the inside of the lid, suggests that these objects belonged to an aristocratic family.

Above: mirror box and incense container. Below: interiors of the mirror box and its lid.

43
Netsuke in box (hako) style

The lid is decorated with three family crests.

Edo period, 18th century.
Dimensions: L 1 ½ in x W 1 ⅜ in x H ¾ in
(3.8 x 3.5 x 1.9 cm)

A *netsuke* is a togglelike object, common in the Edo period, from which objects known as *sagemono* (literally, "hanging things") were suspended from the sashes of men's *kimono*. The free ends of the cord on which the *sagemono* was suspended passed behind the *obi*, or sash, and were fastened to the *netsuke* by means of a concealed knot. The *netsuke* was perched at the top of the *obi*, on the right rear side of the body, where it acted as an anchor to keep the cord from slipping through. In this way the *sagemono*, typically the type of portable container known as an *inrō* (see entry 33), was allowed to hang below the *obi*. The entire ensemble, including the sliding bead (*ojime*) that tightened the cord around the *inrō*, was the focus of an art movement during the Tokugawa period (see entry 55 for an illustration of such an ensemble).

This particular *netsuke* is unusual. About the middle of the sixteenth century a new style of decorative finish was introduced that incorporated the texture of coarse cloth into lacquers. The material served two purposes. It reinforced the underlying wooden form and at the same time allowed the artist a contrasting color and texture to complement the smooth and elegant *maki-e* finish on the rest of surfaces. Lacquer boxes made in this style usually had four fairly large corner areas that revealed this undersurface, lacquered in cinnabar red. Hence this type of box came to be called "red corners" (*sumiaka*).This technique changed little for the next two hundred years, and was usually reserved for large document boxes, because their construction and finish were time-consuming and expensive. *Netsuke* in the *sumiaka* style are extremely rare. The present example was certainly ordered at the whim of some wealthy person.

The outer surface of the lid displays three metallic encrustations, consisting of two family crests, one of them repeated, set in a triangular pattern. The crane crest, at the apex of the triangle, is of silver and probably represents the Mōri family. The two remaining emblems, of gold and silver, are a stylized version of the "three-five" paulownia-blossom crest (*san-go no kirimon*) of the Hosokawa families of Takase or Kumamoto in Kyushu.[51]

The cover and sides of both the lid and bottom of this *netsuke* are finished in sprinkled gold on a black ground. Its construction and decorative finish are of the *sumiaka* style discussed above, along with the typical heart-shaped reserves usually present in boxes of this type. The deep, overhanging lid lifts to reveal an interior finished in heavy *nashiji*.

A metal ring is attached to the center of the inner surface of the lid, and a corresponding hole cut in the bottom of the box. These were used to string the ensemble together as follows. The ends of a silk cord were threaded through the side channels of the *sagemono* and then through the *ojime*. They were then pushed through the hole in the bottom of this box, passed through the metal ring on the inside lid, and knotted. The weight of the suspended object kept the lid secure and the tiny box firmly closed, thus hiding the knot that held it all together.

CONNOISSEURSHIP: This tiny eighteenth-century box is an exact replica of a sixteenth-century design. Because of the techniques involved, this style is almost impossible to fake. Only the *netsuke* format, with its resultant size, tells the viewer that it was made in the eighteenth century.

44
Poetry-slip box (shikishibako)

Decorated in brilliant gold with the family crest of
the Tokugawa.

Edo period, 18th century.
Dimensions: L 9 in x W 8 ⁷⁄₁₆ in x H 2 ⅛ in
(22.9 x 21.4 x 5.4 cm)

Edo-period daimyo had two kinds of possessions. One, *omote dōgu*, included articles necessary for official duties, including weaponry and
other military accoutrements. This term also encom-
passed objects used in the tea ceremony, the accoutrements for the performance of the Noh drama, and
even the libraries of books in Chinese and Japanese.

The second category, *oku dōgu*, consisted of the personal items needed by the lord and all members of his
household, including clothing, household furniture,
and medicines, as well as such items as paintings and
calligraphy that were not intended for official use.[52]
This category also included objects such as the one
shown here, a box made to hold *shikishi*, or poetry
slips. Often such boxes were part of a bride's trousseau and
therefore considered highly personal items.

The box shown here undoubtedly belonged to a
wedding set of a Tokugawa family member. The rich
gold is extraordinarily lavish and the workmanship
superb. Jagged plum branches with oversized blossoms decorate its cover and sides. The effects seen
here are achieved by a variety of techniques, some now
obsolete. After the initial undercoatings of black lacquer were applied, dried, and polished, additional
coats of clear lacquer with an orange tone were laid in.
While they were still sticky, large particles of pure
flaked gold were sprinkled on so heavily that the black
undercoating was completely covered.

The tree trunks were contoured in *sabi urushi*, then
coated in a blend of black and red lacquer, to which

some silver has been added. A thickened layer of lacquer was next laid down in preparation for the application of the gold leaf used in the *hyōmon* technique.
When this was semi-dry and precisely contoured, the
foil forming each of the blossoms was carefully
applied. A tiny knobbed tool employed as a burnisher
then pressed the edges of the petals into place. The
height of elegance and expense was reached when the
surfaces of the golden petals were then further covered—in some instances with finely powdered silver
or orange-tinted gold. Tiny pistils and stamens were
then added to the center of each blossom.

The final step would have been the application of
the *mitsu aoi* or hollyhock emblem, the use of which
was restricted to the Tokugawa family. The form
shown here is the best known of its variants. It appears
five times on the surface of the lid (a symbolic good
luck number) and is repeated three times on each side
(twice on the bottom section and once on the side of
the lid) for a total of seventeen, all displaying subtle
variations in color according to the techniques used.

A matte gold reserve that replicates the edging
found on the poetry slips stored inside surround the
surface design. The interior of the box is covered with
the same heavy sprinkled gold as the outside.

CONNOISSEURSHIP: This design seems surprisingly
modern, considering that it was created in the eighteenth century. The lid may be placed in either of two
directions, with the side motifs remaining continuous.

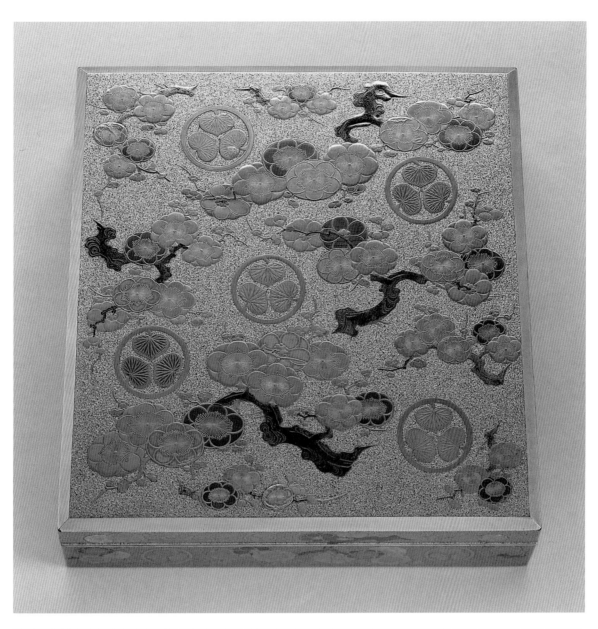

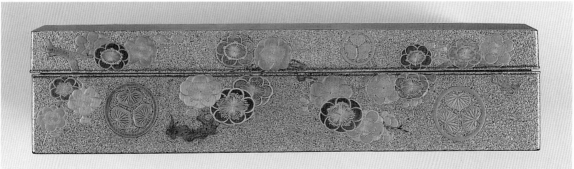

Above: exterior of the box. Below: front panel.

45
Small container (kobako)

Embellished with a repeat pattern of clock faces and chrysanthemum blossoms.

Edo period, 18th century.
Dimensions: L 3 ⅛ in x w 3 ⅛ in x H 2 ¹/₁₆ in
(7.9 x 7.9 x 5.2 cm)

Considering the quality of the gold used on it and its unusual proportions, there is little doubt that this is a special box. Its square shape appears unusually bulky because the lid is one-third of the total height, an atypical proportion for a container of this size and an echo of the sizing of boxes from earlier periods.

The top and four sides are decorated with a repeat pattern consisting of what seems at first glance to be an extrapolation on the design of a Chinese mirror combined with the design of a sixteen-petaled chrysanthemum blossom. Close inspection, however, reveals that each of the mirrorlike patterns is divided into twelve sections. Each section contains a dot signifying one of the twelve divisions of the day (which at that period would have been named after the twelve animals of the Chinese zodiac), and there are tiny arrows in the proper position to signify the four directions. These markings suggest that the pattern is based on an astrological clock.

Arrow-feather designs (*yabane*) connect the clock patterns to each other, and the four directional arrows in each circle point to, but never touch, the chrysanthemum blossoms, which remain suspended against the bright ground. This decoration must have been a tedious undertaking, as each stroke and dot was individually applied without the help of a stencil. The ground consists of a heavy, sparkling *nashiji* on which abundant gold powders were used in *fundame*, enhanced by pure *taka maki-e*. The design flows uninterrupted over the ridges of the cover and continues to the underpart of the bottom section. The edges of the box are lined with lead alloy.

CONNOISSEURSHIP: In Japan, no designs created for boxes were arbitrary, especially one as subtly and carefully finished as this. There was considerable unrest during the later part of the eighteenth century, with the Tokugawa government weakened by widespread corruption. Perhaps this box alludes to the possibility that time was running out for them, and that the imperial family (as represented by the sixteen-petal chrysanthemum), still confined to Kyoto, was waiting for the restoration of its authority (symbolized by the arrow-feather shapes of the connecting design element). Note that the format of the box is not that of an incense container, whose meditative overtones would conflict with the tone expressed in the design on its surfaces.

46
Incense pillow (kōmakura)

Fitted with a drawer on the side designed to hold an incense burner.

Edo period, 18th century.
Dimensions: L 9 ⅛ in x W 4 ½ in x H 4 ⅞ in
(23.2 X 11.4 X 12.4 cm)

Traditionally, the Japanese slept on a matted floor, on which bedding was laid at night, then put away in a closet during the day. During the Edo period, raised pillows on a boxlike wooden frame came into use to protect the elaborate women's hairdos that were then in style. This pillow is a special type, containing a drawer in its side designed to hold a small incense burner. To scent her hair, a woman would rest her head over the open slat-work on the top and back sides of the box, while another special pillow, usually of rolled cloth, supported her neck. This position allowed the perfumed smoke to rise and cling to her hair. The sliding incense drawer was opened and closed by inserting one's finger in a small hole in its face.

The outer surfaces of this pillow are covered with a black lacquer *ro-iro* ground embellished with a hare's-foot fern design in gold *fundame*. Two family crests (*mon*) in different sizes of gold and silver *hira maki-e*, decorate its surfaces, indicating that this object belonged to a highborn family.

The crest with a large central orb surrounded by eight smaller filled circles is called the *kuyō mon* ("nine stars" crest). It is the family crest of the Kitsukawa, the Okudaira of Obata, and the Toda of Ogaki. The other crest, formed by three large comma shapes in a tight circular design turning to the left (*hidari mitsu tomoe*), belongs to the Arima family of Kurume and Fukiage.

The interior and bottom of the box are in *ro-iro*. The side rims, the cutouts on both top and side, and the small pull-hole are all lined in *fundame*.

CONNOISSEURSHIP: Because of the similarity of many crests, care must be taken in identifying them. For example, the *tomoe* design that appears here is spoken of as turning to the left. If it turned right, it would represent a different family.

47
Document or scroll box (fubako)

Decorated with *mon*.

Edo period, late 18th century.
Dimensions: L 9 ½ in x W 2 ⅞ in x H 2 ⅝in
(24.1 x 7.3 x 6.7 cm)

By the end of the eighteenth century, the merchant and artisan classes followed the aristocracy in adopting crests as identifying emblems. It is evident from woodblock prints of famous actors that Kabuki families wore them, and even brothels adopted *mon* to distinguish one house from another. By this time some 4,500 *mon* had been designed, using more than 250 subjects or motifs drawn from the plant and animal kingdoms, as well as assorted popular objects or symbols.

Mon were usually enclosed within a circular border called a surround, although aristocrats did not necessarily employ such a design on objects made for a bride's trousseau. Typically, the emblems of both the bride's family and the family she was joining were displayed (see entries 37 and 38).

This box is covered with a deep-orange-toned, gold-flecked *nashiji* ground, emblazoned with twenty-three crests, of which only one is a duplication. Fifteen of these are on the lid, while eight encircle the bottom part of the box.

The details of each *mon* on this box are rendered in gold *taka maki-e* and *hira maki-e*, while some are further edged in gold (*keuchi*), and embellished with the veining technique of *kakiwari*. The veins of the flowers and delicate touches of orange lacquer within the blazon sharpen the detailing and add both color and textural contrast. A few emblems are rendered in the finely sprinkled matte gold technique of *fundame*, as are all the circular surrounds.

Many of these *mon* are variants on well-known crests belonging to old families, while others originated in the Edo period. The seventeen that can be identified are listed here. The numbers in parentheses correspond to examples of similar crests catalogued in John W. Dower, *The Elements of Japanese Design* (New York and Tokyo: Weatherhill, 1971). The remaining crests are based on types of flowers that cannot be identified with certainty.

1. Wisteria (*fuji*; a variant of the Fujiwara family crest.)[53]
2. Peony (*botan*; 745)
3. Crane (*tsuru*; 1226)
4. Butterfly (*chō*; 1171-1262)
5. Mantled tortoise (*minogame*; 1466)
6. Plum blossom (*ume*; 836-900)
7. Chrysanthemum (*kiku*; 276-325)
8. Bamboo (*take*; 131-90)
9. Orange-blossom tree (*tachibana*; 531-55)
10. Stars (*hoshi*; 101).
11. Water plantain (*omodaka*; 991-1025)
12. Clamshell (*hamaguri*; 1403-25)
13. Helmet shell (*kabutogai*; 1412)
14. Maple leaf (*kaede*; 556-65)
15. Pine tree (*matsu*; 776-85)
16. Passion flower (*tessen*; 656-75)
17. Ivy (*tsuta*; 491)

The interior of the box is finished in a sparse *nashiji*. The metal mounts on the sides, to which cord rings are attached, are in the shape of plum blossoms. The box still retains its silk cords.

CONNOISSEURSHIP: Certain *mon* had such aesthetic appeal that by the late eighteenth century they became generic designs. Intermarriage and the development of branch lineages also led to numerous variations on particular crests. The large number of existing crests and variants created confusion despite attempts at classification and regulation.

The dissemination of heraldic emblems was a sign of the weakening of the class system. A privilege previously extended only to the upper class was now widely available. This box would have been used by a wealthy merchant to store documents. He must have been amused by this expensive object, decorated with hitherto forbidden crests, originally the emblems of his social superiors.

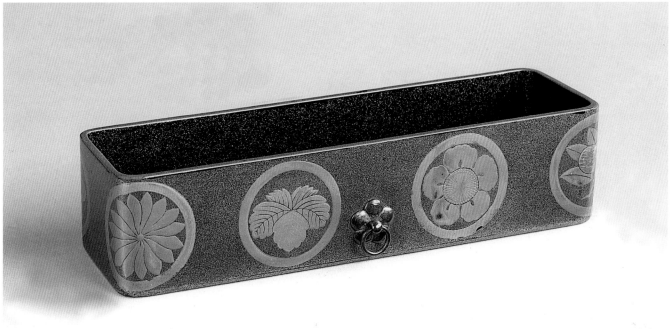

Above: overview of the box. Below: the bottom of the box with the lid removed.

48
Document box (ryōshibako)

Showing a summer waterscape with cranes
and a lotus

Edo period, 18th century.
Dimensions: L 12 ⅜ in x W 10 ⅞ in x H 3 ½ in
(31.4 X 27.5 X 8.9 cm)

W arm summer breezes seem to waft across this idyllic scene. To enjoy it one must enter into the quiet atmosphere of meditation. The Chinese considered the crested crane the patriarch of all birds and the messenger of Taoist holy men. An ancient story maintains that the crested crane was able to live to over six hundred years of age without food, but that it did require water. On this document box two cranes are shown: one in flight and the other on the ground.

A lotus in full bloom emerges from the water in the center of the composition. Respect for this plant is as old as the Indian worship of Brahma, who is sometimes pictured floating on a lotus flower. After his enlightenment the Buddha supposedly saw the lotus as a means to understand the plight of mankind, struggling up through the mud of ignorance. Hence in Buddhism this flower became the symbol of purity.

The center panel of this waterscape is enhanced with a rich *nashiji* border that also separates the four sides of the box into panels. These sections echo the scene on the lid, in which water plantains and bamboo grow in and around a quiet, flowing stream with a faintly suggested shoreline. The techniques seen here, all in various tones of gold, are *togidashi*, with a little *hira maki-e* to provide subtle contrast against the black *ro-iro* ground. The interior of the box is in light *nashiji*.

CONNOISSEURSHIP: The shape of the box is unusual in that it has small recessed feet, an attribute not normally seen on boxes of this type. The religious overtones evident in the box's decorations, coupled with its overall contour, suggesting the shape of a game board, may embody a philosophical comment on the nature of human life.

49
Incense ceremony set
(jūshu kōbako or kōdōgubako)

Arranged in a tiered box with a protective cover in the form of a bird cage.

Edo period, an 18th century "marriage."
Dimensions: L 10 in x W 7 ⅝ in x H 8 ½ in
(25.4 x 19.4 x 21.6 cm)

The incense ceremony (kōdō), or incense game, probably had its origin in the Heian period, when aesthetic skills such as the identification of fragrances became part of the training of aristocrats. Gradually, literary themes became associated with certain fragrances. Sometime in the Muromachi period, the game evolved into a complicated pastime that required a larger variety of scents than used before and accommodated up to ten guests as participants. By the early Edo period, the game reached new heights of popularity, probably as a result of the formalization of the tea ceremony, which also incorporated the burning of incense. During the eighteenth century, possibly because of a shortage of imported scented woods (kōboku), the ceremony survived only among the very rich, and wealthy merchants introduced a modified version of the game and its accoutrements. What follows is a description of the game as it would be played with a set like the one seen here.

The game is customarily played with four fragrances (in the form of pieces of scented wood), three of which are supplied by the host and one by a guest. The three house scents are each divided into four portions, which are placed in individual packets, making a total of twelve packets of house fragrances. The guest fragrance is put into one packet, making a grand total of thirteen.

The game consists of a prelude or preliminary round, during which the three house fragrances are introduced and identified for the players (the guest fragrance remaining a mystery), and the game proper of ten rounds, during each of which the players attempt to identify which of the four possible scents they are currently being given.

In its simplest form, the ceremony's preliminary round begins with the players seated together closely enough for the burning incense to be passed among them easily. The host will have prepared small pieces of burning charcoal beforehand in a larger burner, or kōro (see entry 37). With the proper tool, he lifts a piece of the red-hot charcoal and buries it within the lacquered, ash-filled kikikōro (a special metal-lined container made for this purpose), leaving over it only a thin covering layer of ash. The ash is then smoothed and rounded into a cone with a spatulalike tool.

When the guests appear comfortable, the host opens one packet of the three house fragrances, gives it an identifying name such as "Fragrance One," and then places the perfumed wood on a mica square, which is in turn placed on the heated ash. The burner is then passed around for the guests to acquaint themselves with the fragrance. Fragrance Two and Fragrance Three are introduced and identified in the same manner. After each of the three pieces of incense have been smelled, it is placed on one of a set of plum-blossom-shaped rests that are provided for the purpose. Then the game begins in earnest.

At this point ten packets of fragrance remain— nine of house fragrances and one unknown—and the players will now have to identify them without being told which is which. Each player will have been provided with a set of counters or ballots, all of which will have that player's identifying token (a particular tree or flower) on one side and a possible choice (Fragrance One, Fragrance Two, Fragrance Three, or Unknown Fragrance) on the other. As each new packet is opened and its contents placed in the burner and then passed around, each player chooses a counter that matches his or her guess as to its identity and drops it into a receptacle provided for the purpose. Ten times the burner is passed around and the fragrances inhaled and their identities guessed. Sometimes these actions may be accompanied by a poem or other literary composition characterizing the scent or alluding to the floral motif on the player's ballot. The game becomes increasingly difficult as the closed room fills quickly with lingering aromas from previous rounds.

After each round the ballots are examined, and the players' guesses are written by brush on a record board. (Sometimes the ballots are put in an envelope

Above: the set in its storage cage. Below: top of the storage cage.

Above: the large three-tiered box removed from the cage.
Below: the large tray (kōbon).

until the game is completed and the guesses registered on the board at that time.) The winner is often awarded the record board. Depending on the time available and the number of guests, an intermission may be called and food served in another area.[54]

This particular incense ceremony set is composed of a three-tiered container, enclosed within a cover and base shaped like a bird cage, with bars on all four sides. The outer surface of the lid of the cage is decorated with a sixteenth-century rendition of a flowering paulownia, whose leaves and blossoms are shown scattered to the wind by a powerful unseen force. The silver powders that were applied to some of the leaves and flowers are so worn in certain areas that an undercoating of gold is exposed. This is a rather unique touch, as red or black lacquer is customarily employed as the undercoating for metal powders. Gold *hira maki-e* has been used for edging, contour, and definition. Almost at odds with the composition's feeling of somberness is the freedom of expression visible in the artist's work. There is no doubt that the lid of the cage belonged to an older and much beloved lacquer object. Close examination shows that it has indeed been attached to a previously unrelated piece of wood that reinforces the inner structure of the cage, then refinished to match the other parts of the set. Moreover, it is quite possible that the rest of the cage and its base themselves are of a different period from the fitted, tiered container within. This would mean that at some point in time the bird cage was made using an older lid and that the fittings inside were added even later.

After lifting the barred enclosure from its base (note the four metallic-lacquer edged openings on the sides for fastening it to the base), the three-tiered box can be removed. Inside each of the sections are spaces allocated for the game's accoutrements.

Ginyōban. A compartmentalized tray containing the *honkōban* (see below), usually placed above the *fudabako*.

Honkōban. Customarily ten, but in this particular set thirteen, plum-blossom-shaped rests, made of mother-of-pearl, on which the small mica squares holding the incense are placed after burning. The two cutouts at the center of this tray allow it to be lifted to expose the layer underneath, which contains the *fudabako*.

Fudabako. The tray in which the *kōfuda* are stored.

Kōfuda. The wooden counters or ballots, twelve for each of the ten players. On one side of each ballot is a gold lacquer picture of the plant or tree that will serve as a token for a particular player. The opposite side indicates one of the four possible incense choices (Fragrance One, Two, or Three or Guest Fragrance).

Kirokuban. The record board. This special silver-lacquered tally slate is divided into columns headed by the ten tree or flower names that identify the players. Reading from right to left, these names are *matsu* (pine), *ume* (plum), *sakura* (cherry blossom), *botan* (peony), *tachibana* (orange blossom), *nadeshiko* (fringed pink), *kikyō* (bellflower), *kiku* (chrysanthemum), *momiji* (maple leaf), and *take* (bamboo). The writing on the right side of the board in this example labels it as a record board for the incense game.

Kōbon. A large tray used to display the tools (missing here) for handling the pieces of incense and tending the coals that force the fragrance from the wood. These tools might include a sharp pointed probe for measuring the depth of the ash, a spatula for shaping the ash, chopsticks for lifting the coals, and tongs for placing the fragment of fragrant wood on the mica chip, which is in turn placed on the hot ash. This tray may also hold the burner used for passing the incense around among the players and perhaps a container for the incense itself.

This set includes a tiered incense container (*jūkōgō*), the bottom tier of which is lined with metal to store ash and the other tiers used to store mica

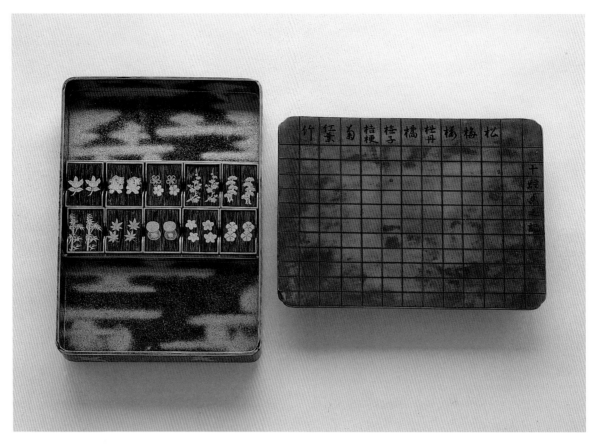

Above: the fudabako, still nested in the large box, and the kirokuban.

Below: components of the set. Clockwise from upper right: the kirokuban, the honkōban, the fudabako, and the jūkōgō.

chips or incense. Other articles usually included, but missing here, are a lacquer box with a slot in in its lid, used to hold the ballots during the round, and paper envelopes that hold the ballots after completion of the round. Almost all the individual lacquer objects in a set like this would be covered with brocade bags for storage at the end of the ceremony.

Images of the night-flying cuckoo (*hototogisu*), a bird often alluded to in Japanese poetry, and said to sing only at the approach of dawn, decorate the outer surfaces of the main three-tiered box, as well as those of the matching tiered incense container inside. Each of the long sides contain thirteen different images of these birds in flight, skillfully drawn in pure gold *taka maki-e* and set against the dramatic jet black of a night sky in which lightly sprinkled gold particles suggest the twinkling of stars. The colorful large tray (*kōbon*) is decorated with a cloudlike ground (*mura nashiji*) against which a flowering plum tree in thick, unadulterated, highly polished gold *taka maki-e* is shown growing over a sectioned fence. The tree matches the theme of the mother-of-pearl incense rests described above, and also serves as an allusion to the "Hatsune" chapter of *The Tale of Genji*. The scene is further decorated with three Chinese characters in silver inlay.

CONNOISSEURSHIP: Incense ceremony sets like the one shown here are now comparatively rare. By the eighteenth century the average aristocrat could no longer afford the outrageously expensive scented woods required for the formal game. Over time, the components of many sets became scattered (see entry 38).

50
Long scroll box (nagafubako)

A stylized floral pattern resembling chrysanthemums and sunflowers covers the lid and base.

Edo period, 18th century.
Dimensions: L 15 ½ in x W2 ¹⁄16 in x H 2 ½ in
(39.4 X 5.2 X 6.4 cm)

This box, like entry 35, is an example of the longer of the two main types of scroll boxes, and more likely to have been used for the storage of a painting or a piece of fine calligraphy than for ordinary scrolled documents such as letters.

Chrysanthemums and sunflowers are central to the design of this container. Fernlike leaves in the shape of curling feathers of gold *hira maki-e* emanate from each blossom, and tiny gold dots or spiral curves completely fill all remaining space. Every surface of the box, including its base, is similarly decorated.

Three things make this box unusual: the attention shown to detail, the way the design fills all available space, and the abstract manner in which the florets have been rendered. This may represent the artist's conception of the mythical Buddhist flower known as the *hosoge*. In boxes from the Nara to Heian periods this blossom is depicted in various ways, but most of the few that are extant show it with multiple curved petals. On these old boxes, made when Chinese influence was at its peak, scrolling, spiral-shaped designs similar to those that appear here also completely occupy the available space. Otherwise there is little similarity in floral imagery between those early boxes and the present one. The latter is separated from them by a thousand years, and during which time Buddhist imagery—based on the imagination—had changed considerably.

The blossoms shown here are of silver, gold, and *e-nashiji* sprinkled powders in *hira maki-e*. Minute particles of cut-gold foil (*kirigane*) have been added to the central parts of some of them. Both the feather-shaped ferns and the tiny scroll and dot designs are made of gold. These images were probably executed with a stencil, the only technique that permits duplication of such fine, clean, and evenly drawn lines. Stencils have been used in lacquer since Kōrin's time (see entry 22) whenever demand necessitated faster production. But they also enabled an artist to create effects impossible without the use of this technique.

The thin lip on the bottom edge of the cover is an indication that this box was made to order. The trilobed cutout that allows for movement of the metal rings is of a slightly flattened design that is unusual in boxes of this type, and further corroborates the idea that this was a special piece. The metal mounts that hold the rings are beautifully crafted as circular twelve-petaled chrysanthemums, echoing the theme on the cover.

The overall quality of this box, the abstract floral imagery, and the special construction employed, hint that this container may have stored some type of Buddhist art.

CONNOISSEURSHIP: In the eighteenth century, sacred relics or sutra fragments owned by devout Buddhist lay persons were probably stored in boxes similar to this. Extant Nara and Heian period sutra boxes were extremely rare, and nearly impossible for an Edo period artist to see. Therefore any attempt to reproduce an image as ancient as the *hosoge* would have had to depend on hearsay and imagination.

51
Tea utensil box (chabako)

Designed for travel. Decorated with a Chinese lion
(*karashishi*) and a peony, in *kamakura-bori*.

Edo period, late 18th century.
Dimensions: L 6 ½ in x W 5 in x H 4 ¾ in
(16.5 x 12.7 x 12.1 cm)

During the Kamakura period the Japanese are
said to have adapted the complicated, heavily
layered red lacquer technique called *tsuishu*,
which was imported from China during the Ming
dynasty (1368–1644). So-called *kamakura-bori* is a simplified version in which wood is carved in relief and
only a few layers of colored lacquer added to finish it.
Popular in the Muromachi period, this style is now
identified more with the city of Kamakura than the
Kamakura period for which it was originally named.

The lid of this wooden box, with its deeply carved
surfaces, displays a bounding image of the imaginary
animal known as the *karashishi*, or Chinese lion. Large
carved images of this mythological animal may be seen
outside many Japanese temples. In art this stylized version of the male lion, the king of beasts, is often associated with the peony (*botan*), the queen of flowers,
representing feminine beauty. Large-petaled peonies

decorate all four sides of the box. The surface of the
inner tray, which was used to hold the accoutrements
stored in the box when tea was served, features shallow carved leaves.

As is typical of the *kamakura-bori* technique, the
bottom layers that cover the wood are made of the
deep red lacquer known as *tsuishu*. One or two skillful
final polishings of the black layers that cover this base
coloring reveals the underlying red. With time and
handling more black will rub off, and the red undercoatings become more visible.

CONNOISSEURSHIP: *Chabako* of the late Edo period in
kamakura-bori are quite rare because they were not considered of great value. They were not Chinese, which
would have made them highly desirable, and they were
not made using gold, which always maintained an
intrinsic value.

The box and its inner tray.

52
Tiered food box (jūbako)

This octagonal Ryukyuan food box with four tiers
and a lid is set within a handled carrier.

Edo period, 18th century.
Dimensions: DIA 7 ⅞ in x H (jūbako only) 10 ¼ in
(20 x 26 cm) H (with carrier) 13 ¾ in (34.9 cm)

The Ryukyu Islands are an arched chain of
islands extending between Kyushu, the
southernmost island of Japan, and Taiwan.
Okinawa is the largest island of the group. By the
fourteenth century, these islands were an independent
kingdom with strong political ties to China. In 1609,
they were invaded by the Japanese domain of
Satsuma, and were officially annexed to Japan in the
early Meiji period (1868–1912).[55] One result of the
seventeenth-century invasion was the interesting
amalgamation of styles that occurred when the
influence of the Japanese aesthetic was added to the
prevailing tradition of artistic influence from China.
Certainly the tiered octagonal shape of the present
box reflects the style of Chinese food boxes from the
Yuan dynasty (1271–1368).

Little is known of the origin of the style of decoration seen here except that there was a mother-of-
pearl inlay factory in Beijing during the fifteenth and
early sixteenth centuries. In 1690 a Japanese named
Seki went to Hangzhou, where he studied the techniques of shell boiling for three years and learned that
by use of this process, thin layers of mother-of-pearl
can be peeled from the otherwise solid, hard shell.[56]
The thinness of these layers increased the brilliance
and iridescence of the material and made it easier to
cut for the inlays used in lacquer objects. Certainly
the eighteenth-century Ryukyuan lacquer design
shown here is a result of this tradition.

This box wonderfully blends Chinese Taoist and
Buddhist themes with motifs of Japanese origin. The
cover and all eight sides are decorated with symbols
associated with these themes. The musical instruments represented include the bell, the conch shell,
the biwa, the koto, and the shō. Taoist imagery is represented by the flute, the fan, the artemisia leaf, and
the scholar's books, examples of the Eight Treasures,
the precious objects associated with the Eight
Immortals of Taoism. A whimsical design flows

around certain of these objects, implying that they
can act as charms.

The iconographic source of the various types of
mollusks and feathers that are interspersed with the
other motifs on the sides may be Chinese. However,
the style of the chrysanthemums placed in the middle
of the cover and scattered on two of the side panels is
purely Japanese. Japanese influence is also reflected on
the side risers, where small patterns of chrysanthemums and hare's-foot fern scrollwork run up and
around the entire surface.

The delicately decorated frame of the bottom section curves into a straight base. By the standards of
Japanese lacquer, the decorations seem somewhat
crude, as the gold has been painted on in the Chinese
manner rather than sprinkled in the Japanese technique of maki-e. Yet each strut of the fans depicted
here has been carefully delineated, with mother-of-
pearl underlying every tiny pattern.

Containers like this were used for special occasions such as festivals in the same manner as the
Japanese sagejūbako (see entry 23). The interiors of all
the tiers and of the cover are in the rich, deep orange
color known as Chinese red or vermilion. The tiered
containers are set in a carrying frame, and a metal bar
is inserted through slots in both sides of the frame to
lock the cover in place. Scroll patterns in an effect
similar to that of gold fundame decorate the sides and
base as well as the underpart of the bottom tier.

CONNOISSEURSHIP: Tiered food containers such as
this are originally thought to have been of Chinese
or possibly of Korean origin since the gold decoration was not applied in maki-e, until the recent
collaboration between Tokugawa Yoshinobu and
Arakawa Hirokazu (then curator of lacquers at the
Tokyo National Museum), which resulted in the
publication of a highly respected book on the art of
Ryukyuan lacquer.[57]

Above: the jūbako in the carrying frame. Below: the frame and the jūbako.

53
Inkstone box (suzuribako)

Decorated with a tiger and cub resting under bamboo leaves.

Edo period, 18th century.
Dimensions: L 9 in x W 8 ½ in x H 2 in
(22.9 x 21.6 x 5 cm)

Tigers are not native to Japan, and therefore pre-nineteenth-century Japanese depictions of this animal were based either on Chinese paintings or pure imagination. Since the subjects displayed both on its exterior and inside allude to ancient legends that would have been known only to scholars, there is little doubt that the present box was made to order for a student of Chinese philosophy.

The large tigress shown here resting near the thick bamboo as she watches her cub would remind the owner of the legend of the mother tiger and her three cubs, two of easy nature and the other contentious. In order to cross a stream for food while keeping the mischievous cub from fighting with his siblings, she contrived to isolate him from the other two. The legend poses a conundrum—how many trips does it take the tigress, carrying one cub at a time, to complete the transfer? The answer, of course, is seven. Here she is resting just prior to leaving on her final trip.

Two stalks of bamboo grow upward on the right side of the image, one smaller than the other. Large pointed leaves jut out over the animals, framing the composition. A few of the large leaves are of pure gold leaf, edged in the *keuchi* style.

The tigress's hunched body is covered with hundreds of curved lines in *taka maki-e fundame* simulating fur. Her nose and eyebrows are of a higher *taka maki-e*, with the mouth lined with *tsuishu*. Her eyes are of inlaid gold leaf (*hyōmon*), with their edges outlined. Stripes have been added in black lacquer to follow her haunches and shoulders, and her paws and sharp claws have been clearly delineated in a realistic manner. The cub's body repeats the same techniques used for the mother.

The interior of the box contains a typical inkstone with a fan-shaped water dropper; a pine tree, mountains, and a small Chinese pavilion decorate the lacquer design on the empty inner tray.

The undersurface of the lid, however, depicts another ancient Chinese legend. According to it, the virtuous sage Hu Yu (known as Kyoyū in Japanese), who was an adviser to the emperor, heard the latter suggest that he might abdicate. To avoid the defilement of hearing such an unthinkable possibility, the sage rushed to the nearest waterfall to cleanse his ears. His close friend Chao Fu (Sōho in Japanese), who understood his companion's sensitive nature, noticed that his ox was drinking downstream and led the animal away from the polluted waters.[58]

One sage's feet are clothed in what the artist must have thought were Chinese slippers. However, having none to copy, he painted them as stockings. The lacing of the sages' caps is in gold leaf, while the body of the ox and the clothing of the men have all been finished in *fundame* and then relacquered with the addition of edging in the *keuchi* style for clean definition.

The upper part of the scene displays a rocky outcrop through which the water falls. Other, smaller bushes have been added beside the pine tree, with minute sprigs of another plant added for interest. The pine needles are in typical *taka maki-e* with tiny pieces of cut gold (*kirigane*) added for textural contrast. These same small square pieces of gold appear under the figures and near the ox to provide highlights and, again, contrast.

CONNOISSEURSHIP: The tiger played an important role in both Taoist lore and Chinese Buddhist iconography, and it became one of the twelve animal signs of the Chinese zodiac. Previously unknown in Japan, the tiger as image and symbol was imported from the continent early in Japanese history, when Japan adopted Buddhism and elements of the Taoist teachings. However, it was not until the eighteenth century that this animal appears in the lacquer arts, and then only in the depiction of Taoist legends or parables.

This box is unique in the detailing of its design and in the rendering of the legend displayed on all its exterior surfaces.

Above: overview of the box. Below: interiors of the box and lid.

54
Small box (kobako)

Decorated with the martial accoutrements of a
mounted samurai.

Edo period, late 18th century.
Dimensions: L 5 ⅜ in x W 4 in x H 1 ⅞ in
(13.7 X 10.2 X 4.8 cm)

The cover of this box is richly decorated in various media and techniques. It features samurai paraphernalia that were symbols of a simpler and more vigorous era when the warrior's life was spent in active service rather than the bureaucratic duties that had become his lot by the latter part of the Edo period.

On a black ground with sprinkled gold particles, the artist has rendered in a literal manner many of the accoutrements that the samurai used for himself and his horse. On the lid a bow and a full quiver are rendered in vermilion *tsuishu*. While both objects are executed in *taka maki-e*, the quiver is further embellished with an edging of dark mother-of-pearl. The saddle's raised texture includes *nashiji*, and its surfaces are decorated in a bamboo pattern.

The helmet, in dark gold *hira maki-e* and *takamaki-e*, is a modified version of the type worn by Minamoto Yoriyoshi (995–1082) during the Heian period.[59] From early times to the late sixteenth century, real antlers were mounted on the helmets of some generals to terrify the enemy; however, metal projections were also utilized for the same purpose, as depicted here. From the metal plates forming the rounded bowl that covers the head, to the cheek protectors, which carry the outline of a family crest, it is evident that the artist used a special model for his work. A heavy silk cord that is threaded through three rings attached on the inside of the helmet ends in tassels which are then tied to secure the helmet from slipping. All these objects have been executed in a gold *taka maki-e* with *kirigane* highlights.

A rope, large ring, and long sword complete the composition on the lid. The four sides of the box are filled with other parts of the samurai's wardrobe and the mountings and other accoutrements of his horse. The front panel shows a *mempō*, a lacquer mask that protected the owner in battle and often resembled his own face. It is finished in raised shiny black lacquer, appearing here in stylized form with the sprinkled gold details of a laced bib and ties. Adjacent to this mask is a tasseled baton, used in battle.

The rear long side of the box includes stirrups in black, gold, and *nashiji*, and a war drum in a blend that uses gold in the *mokume* (simulated woodgrain) technique. The two short sides show a pair of horse's bits (*kutsuwa*) in a metal lacquer finish, and a gold sack with a red drawstring, which is covered in a geometric pattern highlighted in cut gold.

All the design elements are in *taka maki-e* on a sparse *hirame*-sprinkled *ro-iro* ground. Fine, dense *nashiji* coats the interior of the box. The rims and risers are in *fundame*.

CONNOISSEURSHIP: By the end of the eighteenth century, nostalgia for an earlier and presumably more heroic era became the theme of small lacquer boxes such as the one shown here. Especially favored was depiction of the accoutrements of the mounted samurai, including his horse's equipage. Detailed treatment of these objects allowed the artist to show off a variety of difficult lacquer techniques. However, the rather soft quality evident in the rendering here is also indicative of late Edo workmanship.

55
Inkstone box (suzuribako)

The high-domed lid is decorated with two clearly defined *inrō* ensembles on a *wakasa nuri* background.

Edo period, late 18th or early 19th century.
Dimensions: L 9 in x W 8 in x H 2 in
(22.9 x 20.3 x 5.1 cm)

The technique known as *wakasa nuri* is supposed to have originated during the seventeenth century in the Obama area of Wakasa Province in what is now Fukui Prefecture in northern Honshu. Its unusual effect is achieved by applying colored lacquers, principally red, yellow, and brown tones in combination with gold or silver foil on a black base.

Wakasa nuri is made as follows. First a thick ground of a sticky substance such as egg whites, egg shell, or even powdered chalk is deposited on a semi-dry colored-lacquer surface. Then small twigs, pine needles, or rice grains are spread across, and become embedded in the thickened, viscous base. On occasion the technique may be varied by applying such materials as chopped tobacco, seeds, or any other substance the artist may choose. After this base dries, the embedded material is carefully removed to leave a deeply pitted surface which is then covered with various coats of colored lacquers that partially fill in all the tiny pockets.

Next, gold foil is brushed into or on top of the remaining hollow surfaces. This is followed by the addition of several coats of clear lacquer, with polishing in between. This procedure is continued until all the uneven crevices are filled. Finally, after the entire surface is rubbed down to expose the layered colors and gold, the application of a last coat allows the total effect of the underlying design to be seen as if through a clear pool of water.

In the present example, the domed lid of the box has been decorated with two *inrō* ensembles, complete with cord, *ojime*, and *netsuke*. (See entries 34 and 43 for a description of these articles.) The artist who effected the ground used small sprigs of fern combined with straight twigs set in a starlike pattern. Sparsely sprinkled *aogai*, a green-colored shell, was applied before the final coats of clear lacquer were added. The gold and red creates a magnificent backdrop for the two appliqués that further embellish the statement.

In one of the three-piece ensembles, the *inrō*, the ground of which is in black *ro-iro*, displays two colorful cranes amid pine trees. These birds are skillfully executed in silver *togidashi* that also includes other sprinkled colors and gold powders. The *ojime* is an inlay of pure malachite, while the round two-piece netsuke to which it is joined is decorated in gold lacquer.

The second ensemble's *inrō* shows a rooster perched on a drum, with a seated hen beside it (signifying peace). Red, black, and gold-sprinkled lacquers in *taka maki-e* and *hira maki-e* are set off by the *kinji* (shiny gold) ground. The *ojime* inlay is of pure carnelian. The *netsuke*, in the form of a *shishi*, or Chinese lion on a stand, is of carved *tsuishu*. The carefully simulated silk cords that join the three components of each ensemble are of gold lacquer on a *taka maki-e* base.

This bright, elaborate, and very flashy writing box typifies the zenith—and the final phase—in the evolution of lacquer techniques in the period. No doubt this piece was made for a wealthy client as a memento of a special occasion suggested by the subject matter displayed. The use of *wakasa nuri* might be a clue as to the area in which the owner lived. On the other hand, it is possible that its well-known patterning commemorates a visit to the Wakasa area.

Even in its day such a box would have been expensive and tremendously time-consuming to produce. A combination of color and fancifulness like that seen here would have been to the taste of a townsman rather than of a member of the aristocracy.

CONNOISSEURSHIP: The workmanship on the lid is a tour de force of technical prowess and exemplifies the height of artistic achievement in lacquerwork. It is a rare example in perfect condition.

Above: overview of box. Below: detail of the lid.

Appendix

Notes

INTRODUCTION

1. Steven Weintraub, et al., "Urushi and Conservation: The Use of Japanese Lacquer in the Restoration of Japanese Art," p. 41.

2. See Ts'ao T'ien Ch'in, et al., "An Early Medieval Chinese Alchemical Text," p. 152.

3. The *tokonoma* is a decorative alcove equipped with a low shelf, recessed into one wall of the main room of a traditional Japanese house. Usually a painting or piece of calligraphy is hung within the *tokonoma*, and an equally important object, such as a prized ceramic or a lacquered box, is placed on the shelf below.

4. The information and terminology used in this account of lacquer production were supplied to the author by Ōuchi Hachi, owner of the Fujii Urushi Kōgei Company, one of the four remaining *urushiya* in the Tokyo area. He also supplied the photographs shown here.

5. The following description of the techniques used in the construction of lacquer boxes is based on information gathered in the Wajima area of northern Honshu.

6. Langdon Warner, *Japanese Sculpture of the Tempyō Period*, p. 45.

7. See Beatrix von Rague, *A History of Japanese Lacquerwork*, p. 7. This treatise on lacquer was originally published in German in 1967 and remains the most reliable source of information in the field.

8. Equivalent to about ten days wages. Warner, *Japanese Sculpture*, p. 56.

9. Ibid.

10. Warner, pp. 58–59.

11. Arakawa Hirokazu, "Kōgō," pp. 36–39.

12. Wang Shixiang, *Ancient Chinese Lacquer*, p. 191.

13. Wang, pp. 47, 187.

14. The question of whether *byakuro* was really used during the Heian period awaits modern chemical analysis. Recent tests of the metal edging on boxes from the Muromachi and later periods have shown the metal to be lead (see p. 178).

15. von Rague, p. 114.

16. von Rague, p. 258.

17. Only the samurai were allowed to wear two swords. This symbol of their class was abolished after the Meiji Restoration of 1868.

THE COLLECTION

1. Arakawa Hirokazu, "Kōgō," pp. 36–39.

2. Edna S. Levine and William Green, "The Cosmetic Mystique of Old Japan."

3. Ibid.

4. John M. Rosenfield and Shujiro Shimada, *Traditions of Japanese Art: Selections from the Kimiko and John Powers Collection*, p. 190.

5. The metal edges of this and three other boxes in the collection have been tested for their chemical composition by the Bartol Research Institute of the University of Delaware. All of them proved to be composed of lead-based alloys and not pewter, which would contain less than twenty percent lead. See page 178 of this book for the complete chemical analysis.

6. See Barbra Okada, *A Sprinkling of Gold*, p. 93. According to Matsuda Gonroku (1896–1984), who related the story to me directly, the Meiji-era lacquer master Shibata Zeshin rediscovered a similar technique. He used black lacquer and bean curd as the medium, and employed a tool made of whale baleen. In both techniques tiny lumps were left at the edge of the wave pattern as the comb was turned to complete the curve.

7. See Furuto Kazuie, et al., eds. *The Shogun Age Exhibition*, pp. 229, 272.

8. Another possibility is that this scene is an allusion to a mountain called Sue no Matsuyama that often appears as a symbol in classical poetry. Here the implication would be that only a great change could bring waves over this mountain and its pines. See Earl Miner, et al., *The Princeton Companion to Classical Japanese Literature*, p. 439.

9. Donald Keene, *Landscapes and Portraits: Appreciations of Japanese Culture*, p. 22.

10. Kōdaiji is known formally as Kōdaiseijū Zenji. In 1624, Sankō Jōeki, abbot of Kenninji, was appointed founding priest, and Kodaiji became one of the largest and most important subtemples of Kenninji.

11. Air pollution has been a major factor in the deterioration of these pieces, and led to the closing of the Otamaya until restoration can be completed.

12. See Okada Jō, et al. *Nihon no shitsugei*, vol. 2, nos. 89 and 90, for an example of a matching table and inkstone box decorated with a similar pattern.

13. "Calender of Events," *Chanoyu Bulletin*, no. 16 (Fall 1986).

14. A scroll box in the Suntory Museum, undoubtedly by the same artist, is similar in composition and identical in painterly quality and coloring, but without the geometric pattern breaking the design into separate fields. See Suntory Museum of Art, *One Hundred Masterpieces from the Collection of the Suntory Museum of Art*, p. 74.

15. Yoshimura Moto, *Kōdaiji maki-e*, p. 25.

16. Ibid., p. 40. This is a different box from the one mentioned in footnote 14, which is a *fubako*, and does not share the broken pattern.

17. Burton Watson, ed. and trans., *The Columbia Book of Chinese Poetry*, p. 135. Another translation of the same phrase reads, "I pick chrysanthemums by the Eastern Gate." See Andrew Pekarik, *Japanese Lacquer, 1600–1900*, p. 28

18. A scroll box with a similar design of clematis, but with an additional family crest, may be seen in Okada, *Sprinkling of Gold*, p. 40.

19. One translator of the text from the classical Japanese states that "there are three relationships which must be understood in order to appreciate *Tales of Ise.* These are the relationships between man and nature, man and court society, and man and woman." H. Jay Harris, trans., *Tales of Ise*, p. 24.

20. See Helen Craig McCullough, trans., *Tales of Ise*, p. 75. The apparent mismatch between the fourth syllable (*ba*) and the fourth line of the poem, which begins *ha*, would not be confusing in the Japanese writing system, where both would be written with the same *kana* character.

21. Laurel Rodd, with Mary Henkenius, trans., *Kokinshū*, p. 307.

22. For similarly constructed boxes attributed to Hon'ami Koetsu in both the Charles A. Greenfield collection and that of the Atami Art Museum in Japan, see Andrew Pekarik, *Japanese Lacquer*, pp. 56, 58.

23. Rodd, *Kokinshū*, p. 109.

24. For a similar example of a repeat pattern using two sets of flowers within a medallion, see James C. Y. Watt and Barbara Brennan Ford, *East Asian Lacquer*, p. 245.

25. Okada, *Sprinkling of Gold*, p. 50, note 2.

26. Kurt Herberts, *Oriental Lacquer*, p. 378.

27. Present-day *tsugaru nuri* does not usually include mother of pearl, silver powders, or the depth of patterning in evidence here.

28. Masaki Naohiko, "Haryū zaiku no hanashi," pp. 1–2.

29. See Mikami Tsugio, *The Art of Japanese Ceramics*, pp. 169–74, for a discussion of this subject.

30. I would like to thank Yasuhiro Nishioka, head curator of the Department of Oriental Antiquities at the Tokyo National Museum, and his staff, for their transliteration and translation and of this poem. Hideo and Reiko Suzuki of Tokyo also provided valuable assistance.

31. The year is given in two Chinese characters representing elements in a cycle of sixty years, and always corresponds to one of the twelve animal signs in the Chinese zodiac—in this case, the sheep.

32. The original box is in the collection of the Tokyo National Museum.

33. Helen Craig McCullough, *Brocade by Night*, p. 323.

34. For further discussion of the theme of the Uji Bridge, see Mieko Murase, *Japanese Art*, pp. 160–63.

35. For a complete chemical analysis of this alloy, see p. 178 below.

36. Examples of *inrō* designs from this period may be found in Inaba Shin'uemon, *Soken kishō*, pp. 18–19.

37. For an example of such depictions see Okada, *Real and Imaginary Beings*, p. 16, fig. 4.

38. Even today, traditional patent medicines are still considered effective by many Japanese.

39. Okada, *Real and Imaginary Beings,* figs. 5 and 6.

40. Kurt Herberts. *Oriental Lacquer,* p. 392.

41. John Dower, *The Elements of Japanese Design.* p.3.

42. Dower, p. 4.

43. Okada Jō, et al., *Nihon no shitsugei,* vol. 2, nos. 89–90, 102.

44. Yoshimura, *Kodaiji maki-e,* p. 16.

45. Yoshimura, p. v.

46. *Chanoyu Quarterly,* no. 25 (1980), p. 49.

47. In identifying a family crest, many elements must be considered. The type of object represented is the first consideration (in this case, the shape of the feathers). Second is the number of objects, their relation to each other, and finally, their orientation. In this case there are two feathers, with the one in front crossing from right to left and the other in back, slanting left to right.

48. For other such "marriages" see entries 23 and 49.

49. Translation by Sonja Arntzen, in *Chanoyu Quarterly,* no. 28 (1981), p. 47.

50. Transcribed from *sōsho* script by Nakai Tobo of Osaka with the help of Imakoji Yuko of Kyoto, the poem reads as follows in Japanese:

    Saburai no
    Kawarade toshi no
    Tsumore ka shi
    Tatoi inochi wa
    Kagiri aru tomo

    The paraphrase in the text is by Reiko Suzuki of Tokyo.

51. Stylized crests like these are very difficult to identify. By the eighteenth century, these heraldic emblems had become so popular that innumerable variations appeared, with each distant branch of the main family striving for its own identifying mark.

52. For more detailed treatment of this subject, see the essay by Tokugawa Yoshinobu in Furuto Kazuie, et al., eds. *The Shogun Age Exhibition,* pp. 28–31.

53. Victor F. Weber, *Koji hōten,* vol. 2, pp. 68–69. For other crests see pp. 66–89.

54. I would like to thank Yaegashi Naoko of New York for her help in providing research materials and information regarding the objects used in the incense ceremony.

55. After the invasion by Satsuma, a treaty between Satsuma and the Ryūkyū kingdom in 1611 preserved the "independence" of the latter, though under Satsuma's overlordship. The islands were not formally annexed to Japan until after the Meiji Restoration. For other information on this subject, see James Watt and Barbara Ford, *East Asian Lacquer,* pp. 326–71.

56. Lee Yu-Kuan, *Oriental Lacquer Art,* pp. 270–71.

57. Arakawa Hirokazu and Tokugawa Yoshinobu, *Ryūkyū shikkōgei.*

58. Henri L. Joly, *Legend in Japanese Art,* pp. 276–77.

59. The well-known *Heike monogatari* (Tale of the Heike) relates the events of the final days of the conflict between the Taira and Minamoto families. Following the last battle in 1185, the Minamoto won control of the country, inaugurating the era of samurai rule and ending the court-centered Heian period.

Provenance of Selected Boxes from the Collection

ENTRY 12.

Fubako (document box): Autumn flowers and grasses, paulownia and chrysanthemum crests.

Collection: Michael Dean.

Published: Michael Dean, *Japanese Lacquer: An Exposition by M & H Dean* (Tokyo: Kyoto Shoin, 1984), no. 31.

ENTRY 13

Kagamibako (mirror box): Chrysanthemums and fence.

Exhibited: The Newark Museum, 1983; Lowe Art Museum, University of Miami, 1985.

Published: Barbra Teri Okada, *A Sprinkling of Gold* (Newark: The Newark Museum, 1983), entry 5, p. 39.

ENTRY 17

Suzuribako (inkstone box): Chrysanthemums at night.

Collection: Charles A. Greenfield.

Exhibited: The Metropolitan Museum of Art, New York, 1980.

Published: Andrew Pekarik, *Japanese Laquer 1600–1900: Selections from the Charles A. Greenfield Collection* (New York: The Metropolitan Museum of Art, 1980), pp. 19–20, figs. 9 and 11; Eskenazi & Co., *The Charles A. Greenfield Collection of Lacquer* (London: 1990), pp. 36-37.

ENTRY 25

Suzuribako (inkstone box): Chinese sage.

Collection: Aoyama.

Published: "Reach—Japanese Beauty and Heart." A Japanese film on the Ehrenkranz Collection produced by Kiwameru for Tokyo Television (Channel 10), 1993.

ENTRY 26

Suzuribako (inkstone box): Tasseled mirror and hydrangea.

Collections: Arthur Kay; Virginia Atchley.

ENTRY 29

Suzuribako (inkstone box): Eight-paneled screen.

Collection: Henri Vever.

ENTRY 30

Suzuribako (inkstone box): Open fan showing a monkey on a persimmon tree.

Collections: Roman Vishniac; Lady Lawrence.

Published: Henry L. Joly and Kumasaku Tomita, *Japanese Art and Handicraft* (The Red Cross Catalogue of 1915), Plate LXIX, no. 53.

ENTRY 39

Chasenzutsu (tea whisk container): Paulownia-blossom crest.

Collection: Mary Louise O'Brien.

ENTRY 43

Box-style *netsuke:* Three family crests (*mon*).

Collection: Mary Louise O'Brien.

ENTRY 44

Shikishibako (poetry-slip box): Flowering plum-tree and the family crest of the Tokugawa.

Collections: Samuel T. Peters; Charles A. Greenfield.

Exhibited: The Japan House, New York, 1972; Frederick S. Wright Art Gallery, University of California, Berkeley, 1976; Asia House Gallery, New York, 1977; The Metropolitan Museum of Art, New York, 1980.

Published: Harold P. Stern, *The Magnificent Three: Lacquer, Netsuke and Tsuba,* (New York: Japan Society, 1972), no. 46; Harold P. Stern, *Birds, Beasts, Blossoms, and Bugs,* (New York: Harry N. Abrams, 1976), no. 126; Andrew Pekarik, *Japanese Lacquer 1600–1900: Selections from the Charles A. Greenfield Collection* (New York: The Metropolitan Museum of Art, 1980), p. 128, fig. 150.

ENTRY 45

Kobako (small container): Repeat pattern of clocks and chrysanthemum blossoms.

Collection: John H. Webster.

ENTRY 53

Suzuribako (inkstone box): Tigress and cub.

Published: Barbra Teri Okada, *A Sprinkling of Gold* (Newark: The Newark Museum, 1983), p. 135, fig. 1.

ENTRY 55

Suzuribako (inkstone box): Two *inrō* on a *wakasa nuri* ground.

Collection: Virginia Atchley

Chemical Analysis of Metal Furnishings on Five Japanese Boxes

For centuries art historians have disputed whether the gray metal edging various lacquer boxes is pewter or lead. Considerable conflict has also arisen over the composition of metal inlays. Until recently, judgment rested primarily on visual observation, but the advent of spectrographic analysis has made possible much more precise determination. In the interests of scholarship, Elaine Ehrenkranz sent four of her boxes and a piece of inlay from a fifth to the Bartol Research Institute at the University of Delaware, where they were analyzed by Dr. Charles P. Swann. He concluded that the metal edging on the boxes and their lids is a lead-based alloy, while the inlay is of nearly pure silver. According to Dr. Swann: "All edgings are lead-based alloys…the material is not pewter: pewter would have less than twenty percent lead." Although the results shown below are of course limited to the boxes tested, it seems likely that edging of similar tone and texture on other boxes of the period is of the same composition found here.

Element	Box	Lid
Entry 1		
Fe (Iron)	0.18	0.14
Cu (Copper)	0.85	1.08
As (Arsenic)	0.96	0.56
Ag (Silver)	2.69	0.56
Sn (Tin)	11.53	18.08
Sb (Antimony)	0.13	0.12
Pb (Lead)	83.63	79.15
Entry 16		
Fe	0.19	0.12
Cu	1.24	1.06
As	0.96	0.99
Ag	0.03	0.04
Sn	1.68	1.68
Sb	0.12	0.07
Pb	95.82	95.98
Entry 36		
Fe	0.15	0.16
Cu	1.02	1.29
As	0.76	1.00
Ag	0.30	0.18
Sn	23.28	14.38
Sb	0.92	1.08
Pb	73.71	81.85

Element	Box	Lid
Entry 45		
Fe	0.11	0.12
Cu	0.70	0.72
As	1.15	1.29
Ag	0.39	0.13
Sn	44.45	42.99
Sb	0.16	0.15
Pb	53.05	54.49

For the following entry, a small piece of metal inlay in the form of a cherry blossom was tested.

Element	Box
Entry 28	
Fe (Iron)	0.04
Cu (Copper)	0.74
Au (Gold)	0.12
Pb (Lead)	0.14
Bi (Bismuth)	0.04
Ag (Silver)	98.92

Glossary

The lacquer terms listed below are derived from a variety of sources (see bibliography), and from direct observation. The most complete description of lacquer terms available in English may be found in Kurt Herberts, *Oriental Lacquer*.

agemuro—A low-humidity chamber for the curing of freshly lacquered objects.

akagane nuri—The fox-red metallic finish that results when a special mixture or "pickle" is applied to a copper alloy base. The chemical reaction forms a skin on the exposed surface. This skin is then scraped off and the resulting powder sprinkled on wet lacquer.

aogai—Abalone shell. A blue-green iridescent shell, sometimes also marked with red, used in inlay work since the seventeenth century.

aokin fun—A gold powder with a bluish cast, the result of mixing silver powders into it.

byakuro—A greyish-white alloy similar to pewter.

chinkinbori—A technique in which lines are engraved in a lacquered surface, then lightly lacquered and filled with gold powder or foil, so that the incised design is clearly revealed.

chōshitsu—A Chinese method of carving multilayered lacquer (see *tsuishu* and *tsuikoku*).

dakkan shitsu—A sculpture technique used in the Nara period. A mold was taken of a clay image; the clay image was removed and the inside of the mold was coated with lacquer, bark, and cloth soaked in lacquer. After this hardened, the mold was broken away, leaving the dried-lacquer figure to be polished and decorated.

e-nashiji—This term is used when the "pear-skin" ground (*nashiji*) technique has been employed in the pictorial elements, rather than as the overall ground of the composition. Widely used during the Momoyama period, this technique fell into disuse around the end of the seventeenth century.

e-urushi—A combination of *suki urushi* and the red coloring matter known as *bengara*, used for underdrawings. After

this mixture was applied in a pattern, gold powders were sprinkled over the semi-dry lines. When dry, the red undercolor lent a reflective tone and richness to the gold powders on its surface.

fundame—Heavily sprinkled gold powder composed of particles so fine that its surface cannot be polished. The surface obtained remains matte or dull in appearance compared with those made of more coarsely ground powder.

furo—A wet box, or wooden chamber for "curing" lacquer objects. Its interior is sprayed with water, or wet cloths are hung inside it to provide the necessary 80 to 85 percent humidity required for the hardening of lacquer.

harigaki, *haribori*, or *hikkaki*—A design technique of the Momoyama period in which a needle or other pointed instrument, such as a sharpened quill, is used to scratch through the gold decoration on a black lacquered surface to expose the color of the ground.

heidatsu—(sometimes used interchangeably with the term *hyōmon*). An appliqué technique using sheet gold or silver. After coating the metal with layers of lacquer, the surface is then rubbed down with abrasives to expose only the metal appliqué.

hiramaki-e—Known as low relief, this technique was introduced in the Kamakura period. A single layer of lacquer is applied to the ground, sprinkled with gold or silver powders, and allowed to dry. A coat of thin lacquer is then applied to fix the the particles, and given a final polish.

hirameji—A technique in which irregularly shaped, flattened flakes of gold are sprinkled sparingly over a moist black lacquer ground. When dry, the surface is recoated several times with clear lacquer, then partially re-exposed by polishing. Some sources state that examples of this method were termed *heijin* from the ninth and tenth century. This technique stems from the Kamakura period. There is also some doubt as to whether this procedure involved sprinkling, rather than placing each particle individually into the wet ground (see *oki hirame*).

hyōmon—Sometimes termed "sheet design." In this technique a figure or pattern is cut from thin sheets of metal and pasted on a finished surface. After several clear coats of lacquer are applied, the surface above the metal design is polished or scraped away, exposing the pure color of the metal (see *heidatsu,* above).

ikakeji—A process in which a ground is created by the heavy sprinkling of gold or silver powder in a single coat. *Ikakeji* was the precursor of *fundame,* which was followed in the nineteenthth century by *kinji.*

inrō—A portable, tiered medicine container worn suspended from the sash of the kimono. Originally these objects are thought to have functioned as cases for the owner's personal seal and ink, and some *inrō* so equipped are still extant.

ippenji nuri—The first-ground coating of lacquer used to seal the core or form of a lacquer box.

iro-e togidashi—A technique in which pigments, including gold or silver powders, are used for creating the pictorial image. After the pigments have been sprinkled on a wet ground, the sprinkled picture is then covered with repeated layers of lacquer, usually black. The surface is then polished down until the picture is revealed (see *togidashi*).

jinoko—A special clay found in the Wajima area of the Noto Peninsula. After processing, it is suspended in a lacquer medium and used for sealing the core of an object before decorative lacquer designs are applied.

kagamibako—Mirror box. The storage box for a round metal mirror.

kakigama—An instrument used for scoring tree trunks in order to collect *urushi.*

kakihera—A curved instrument for scraping away the *urushi* that has been exuded by the tree after cutting.

kakiwari—A technique in which a design element, such as the veining of a leaf, is left in reserve, allowing the background to provide the contrast.

kamakura-bori—A lacquer technique supposedly named after the Kamakura period (1185–1333), when it was introduced, but now referring to the city of Kamakura. Wood is carved in relief, and then usually covered with black lacquer, followed by red, which is than rubbed down, revealing the subtle color underneath. *Kamakura-bori* was invented to resemble the more difficult and time-conuming Chinese lacquer-carving techniques known as *tsuishu* and *tsuikoku.*

kanagai—A technique in which sheet metal (usually gold) was cut into various sizes and applied as decorative highlights, in much the same manner as *heidatsu* or *hyōmon.*

kanshitsu—Dry lacquer.

kashibako—A container for storing sweets for the tea ceremony.

katami-gawari—A Momoyama design motif resembling a lightning bolt.

keuchi—A type of *hiramaki-e* technique. The edges of leaves, flowers, or other design elements are emphasized with an additional layer of sprinkled gold powder, giving an outline effect.

kiji—The core, form, or base of a lacquer object, usually made of wood.

kingin-e—A technique in which powdered gold or silver is mixed with glue used in rendering a design.

kinji—A heavily sprinkled, powdered-gold ground that takes on a shiny finish when polished. This technique was introduced in the late Edo period.

kirigane—A decorative technique employing tiny pieces of gold leaf cut in various shapes, sometimes forming a kind of mosaic.

ki shōmi (or *kijōmi*) *urushi*—Unprocessed Japanese *urushi* from the middle trunk of the tree.

kō—Incense.

kobako—Small box.

kōbako—Incense box. Usually larger than a *kōgō.*

kōdansu—A portable drawered cabinet for the storage of accoutrements for the incense game.

kōdō—The incense ceremony or incense game. Literally, "The Way of Incense."

kōdōgubako—A box for incense ceremony implements.

kōgō—Incense container.

kojūbako—A small tiered covered container for holding incense and other small objects used in the incense game, such as mica.

kurome—The term applied to the heating process in the refining of lacquer by which excess water is removed from the sap.

kuro urushi—Black urushi. The dark, lower-quality lacquers to which black is added in the form of iron powder or filings before heat is applied.

maki-bokashi—A term applied to the application of sprinkled gold powder to form a tonal gradation.

maki-e—The technique of sprinkling metallic or pigmented powders on a wet lacquer ground to form a composition or design.

maki-e shi—The lacquer artist who creates and finishes the surface design elements.

makihanashi—A Momoyama technique in which the design is executed in sprinkled gold and does not receive a final polishing.

makkinru—The precursor of the burnished *maki-e* technique known as *togidashi*.

matsukawa-bishi—An early design motif resembling the bark of a pine tree. This motif was first introduced in the Muromachi period but is more commonly found in Momoyama lacquers.

mura nashiji—A technique in which the application of *nashi-ji* simulates the appearance of floating clouds.

naka nuri—Middle undercoatings applied to the core or form of a lacquer box, utilizing black *urushi*.

nashiji—(literally, "pear-skin ground"). So named because small, irregular gold flakes are sprinkled in several layers in an orange-toned lacquer medium, which is then polished to resemble the skin of a Japanese pear (*nashi*).

nashiji urushi—A transparent lacquer with a yellow-orange color achieved through the addition of a powdered resin called *shiō*.

nihenji nuri—The second-ground coat applied to the core or form of a lacquer object. A mixture of medium-grade baked clay combined with *urushi* .

nuritate—An unpolished final coating of black lacquer, with oil added, used as an undecorated surface finish on the insides and bottoms of many boxes created from the Taishō period onward.

oki hirame—Large, irregular gold flakes, usually placed separately on a finished surface and then covered with a final coat of lacquer. It is sometimes confused with Gyōbu *hirame*, the difference being that in the latter, the gold flakes are generally suspended in *nashiji urushi*.

raden—Mother-of-pearl.

ro-iro—A technique using the highest quality black *urushi*, applied in several layers. Polishing and grinding is required after each layer, resulting in a shiny black waxy ground. It is only used on the highest quality boxes.

ryōshibako—Document box. A box for storing papers or stationery.

sabi urushi—A thick paste made by kneeding pumice, *urushi*, and water. The resultant material is used to build *taka-maki-e*.

sagedansu—A portable cabinet.

sagejūbako—A portable, tiered lunch box set.

sanbenji nuri—The third and final ground applied to the core or form of lacquer boxes.

seisei urushi—The term applied to processed cooked lacquer.

shakudō nuri—An alloy of copper and gold that when placed in a solution or "pickle, " forms a black or sometimes purple-colored skin. This skin is then scraped off and the resultant powder sprinkled on wet lacquer.

shibo urushi—A process in which black lacquer is combined with a stiffening agent, such as bean curd.

shiō—Gamboge. A gum-tree resin that is bright yellow in powdered form.

shitaji nuri—The primary undercoatings applied to the core or form of a lacquer box.

shu—Cinnabar. Used as a red coloring material in lacquer.

shuai urushi—A compound made by adding cinnabar to plain oil urushi.

suke urushi—Plain lacquer to which light coloring material or oil may be added.

suki—Processed plain lacquer.

suri urushi—A wash of thin lacquer usually added to "fix" metal or colored powders more firmly to the ground before polishing.

suzuribako—Inkstone box. A fitted box containing writing implements such as an inkstone, a water dropper, and brushes.

taka maki-e—Known as high relief, this technique involves building up a design using two or more layers of lacquer or lacquer compounds. The final surface is usually decorated.

tebako—Literally, "hand box," this container was used to store cosmetics, and takes its name from the fact that it was small enough, presumably, to be easily held in a lady's delicate hands.

tetsusabi nuri—A technique simulating a rusted iron finish.

togidashi maki-e—A technique also known as "burnishing." The design is first drawn on a ground in wet lacquer, then metallic or pigmented powders are sprinkled over the moist composition. When the surface is completely dry, additional layers of black lacquer are added to coat this surface, thus building up infinitesimally small mounds. The surface is then carefully ground down until the original sprinkled design is revealed.

tomobako—The original wooden box in which an object is stored after completion by the artist. It usually has an inscription on the lid and is signed on the inside.

tonoko—Pulverized pumice.

tsugaru nuri—A style of lacquer associated with the ancient province of Tsugaru in the northern part of the island of Honshū.

tsuikoku or *tsuishu*—The Chinese-derived method of applying and then carving multilayered lacquer, either black (*koku*) or red (*shu*).

urushiya—A processing plant and storehouse for lacquer; an importer from which lacquer stores buy their supplies; a place that sells lacquer.

uwa nuri—The final, top coatings applied to the core or form of a lacquer object.

wakasa nuri—A style of lacquer associated with the province of Wakasa.

yasurifun—Coarse filings produced by rubbing a file over a piece of gold.

Bibliography

"A Lacquer Box." *Kokka*, no. 228 (May 1909): pp. 359-62.

Aimi Kōu. "Kankō geijutsu to Haryū" [Haryū and the art of inlay]. *Nihon Bijutsu Kyōkai Hōkoku*, no. 33 (July 1934); no. 34 (October 1934); no. 36 (April 1935); no. 37 (July 1935).

Arakawa Hirokazu. "Maki-e." *Nihon no Bijutsu*, no. 35 (March 1969).

———. "Kōgō" [Incense boxes]. *Pyramid* (November 1977).

———. *Shitsu kōgei* [Lacquerwork].Tokyo: Hoikusha, 1982.

——— and Tokugawa Yoshinobu. *Ryūkyū shikkōgei* [Lacquerwork of the Ryūkyūs]. Tokyo: Nihon Keizai Shimbunsha, 1977.

———, et al. *Kachō: Bird and Flower Motifs*. Traditions in Japanese Design. Tokyo: Kodansha International, 1967.

Art Institute of Chicago. *The Great Eastern Temple: Treasures of Japanese Buddhist Art from Todai-ji*. Chicago, 1986.

Bedford, John. *Chinese and Japanese Lacquer*. New York: Walker and Company, 1969.

Blakemore, Frances. *Japanese Design Through Textile Patterns*. New York & Tokyo: Weatherhill, 1978.

Boger, H. Batterson. *The Traditional Arts of Japan*. Garden City: Doubleday & Company, 1964.

Boyer, Martha. *Japanese Export Lacquers from the Seventeenth Century in the National Museum of Denmark*. Copenhagen: The National Museum, 1959.

Breuer, A. A. *The Influence of China on Lacquer in Japan*. London: Translations of the Japan Society, 1914.

Brower, Robert, and Earl Miner. *Japanese Court Poetry*. Stanford: Stanford University Press, 1961.

Bunkachō [Agency for Cultural Affairs]. *Mukei bunkazai kiroku, kōgei gijutsu hen 4: Maki-e* [Record of intangible cultural properties, handicraft techniques, vol. 4: *maki-e*]. Tokyo: Daiichi Hōki Shuppan, 1973.

Castile, Rand. *The Way of Tea*. New York & Tokyo: Weatherhill, 1971.

Chanoyu Bulletin, no. 16 (Fall 1986).

Chanoyu Quarterly: Tea and the Arts of Japan. Kyoto: Urasenke Foundation, 1976–86.

Dean, Michael. *Japanese Lacquer: An Exposition by M & H Dean*. Tokyo: Kyoto Shoin, 1984.

Dower, John W. *The Elements of Japanese Design*. New York & Tokyo: Weatherhill, 1971.

Fujioka Ryoichi. *Tea Ceremony Utensils*. Translated and adapted by Louise Allison Cort. New York & Tokyo: Weatherhill, 1973.

Furuto Kazuie, et al., eds. *The Shogun Age Exhibition from the Tokugawa Art Museum*. Tokyo: The Shogun Age Exhibition Executive Committee, 1983.

Gabbert, Gunhild. *Ostasiatische Lackkunst* [East Asian lacquer art]. Frankfurt am Main: 1978.

———. *Buddhistische Plastik aus China und Japan* [Buddhist sculpture of China and Japan]. Wiesbaden: 1972.

Gōke Tadaomi. "Kamakura-bori." *Nihon no Bijutsu*, no. 70 (February 1972).

Harris, H. Jay, trans. *The Tales of Ise*. Rutland, Vermont & Tokyo: Charles E. Tuttle, 1972.

Hayashiya Seizō. *Chanoyu: Japanese Tea Ceremony*. Translated and adapted by Emily J. Sano. New York: Japan Society, 1979.

Herberts, Kurt. *Oriental Lacquer: Art and Technique*. London: Thames and Hudson, 1962.

Impey, Oliver. "Japanese Export Lacquer of the Seventeenth Century," in William Watson, ed., *Lacquerwork in Asia and Beyond*. Colloquies on Art and Archeology in Asia, no. 11. London: Percival David Foundation of Chinese Art, 1982.

Inaba Shin'uemon. *Sōken kishō*, vol. 6. Osaka: 1781

Jahss, Melvin and Betty. *Inrō and Other Miniature Forms of Japanese Lacquer Art*. Rutland, Vermont & Tokyo: Charles E. Tuttle, 1971.

Japanese Lacquer Art: Modern Masterpieces. Translated by Richard L. Gage. New York & Tokyo: Weatherhill, 1982.

Japan Society and the Suntory Museum of Art, Tokyo. *Autumn Grasses and Water: Motifs in Japanese Art from the Suntory Museum of Art.* New York: Japan Society, 1983.

Joly, Henri L. *Legend in Japanese Art.* 1908. Reprint, Tokyo: Charles E. Tuttle, 1967.

Kageyama Haruki and Christine Guth Kanda. *Shinto Arts: Nature, Gods, and Man in Japan.* New York: Japan House Gallery, 1976.

Kaiyama Kyūsaburō. *The Book of Japanese Design.* Translation and commentary by Sylvia Price Mueller. New York: Crown, 1969.

Kawahara Masahiko. *Ninsei.* Nippon tōji zenshū, vol. 27. Tokyo: Chūō Kōronsha, 1976.

Keene, Donald. *Landscapes and Portraits: Appreciations of Japanese Culture.* Tokyo: Kodansha International, 1971.

Kodansha Encyclopedia of Japan. 9 vols. Tokyo & New York: Kodansha, 1983.

Kodansha. *Japan: An Illustrated Encyclopedia.* 2 vols. Tokyo & New York: Kodansha, 1993.

Kōdō Nyūmon [Introduction to the incense ceremony]. Tankō Mook Series. Kyoto: Tankōsha, 1993.

Kokin Wakashū [Poems ancient and modern]. Nihon koten bungaku taikei, vol. 12. Tokyo: Iwanami Shoten, 1958.

Kyoto National Museum. *Tokubetsuten: Momoyama jidai no kōgei* [Special exhibition: Handicrafts of the Momoyama period]. Kyoto: Kyoto National Museum, 1975.

———. *Kōgei ni miru koten bungaku ishō* [The world of classical Japanese literature as reflected in handicrafts]. Kyoto: Kyoto National Museum, 1980.

Lee, Sherman. *Japanese Decorative Style.* Cleveland: The Cleveland Museum of Art, 1961.

———. *The Genius of Japanese Design.* Tokyo: Kōdansha International, 1981.

Lee, Yu-Kuan. *Oriental Lacquer Art.* New York & Tokyo: Weatherhill, 1972.

Levine, Edna S. and William Green. "The Cosmetic Mystique of Old Japan." *Impressions* 4 (Winter 1980).

Masaki Naohiko. "Haryū zaiku no hanashi" [Reminiscences of Haryū]. *Tokyo Bijutsu Gakkō kōyūkai geppō* 9 (April 1930).

Matsuda Gonroku. *Urushi no Hanashi* [Speaking of lacquer]. Iwanami Shinsho, no. 542. Tokyo: Iwanami Shoten, 1977.

McCullough, Helen Craig, trans. *Tales of Ise: Lyrical Episodes from Tenth-Century Japan.* Stanford: Stanford University Press, 1968.

———. *Brocade by Night: Kokin Wakashū and the Court Style in Japanese Classical Poetry.* Stanford: Stanford University Press, 1985.

———, trans. *Kokin Wakashū: The First Imperial Anthology of Japanese Poetry.* Stanford: Stanford University Press, 1985.

Mikami Tsugio, *The Art of Japanese Ceramics.* Tokyo & New York: Weatherhill, 1972.

Miner, Earl, et al. *The Princeton Companion to Classical Japanese Literature.* Princeton: Princeton University Press, 1985.

Mitsukuni Yoshida. *The People's Culture from Kyoto to Edo.* Hiroshima: Mazda Motor Corporation, 1986.

Mizoguchi Saburō. "Bijutsu yōgo (shikkō): togidashi maki-e" [Art terminology (lacquer): *togidashi maki-e*]. *Museum*, no. 23 (February 1953).

———. *Design Motifs.* Arts of Japan, vol. 1. Translated and adapted by Louise Allison Cort. New York & Tokyo: Weatherhill, 1973.

Mizuuchi Kyōhei. *Cha no shikki* [Lacquerware for tea]. Kyoto: Tankōsha, 1981.

Moriya Kenrō, ed. *Nihon no shikkō* [Japanese lacquer]. Tokyo: Yomiuri Shimbunsha, 1979.

Muraoka Hiroshi. *The Awakening of Japan.* Tokyo: Kenkyūsha, 1940.

Murasaki Shikibu. *The Tale of Genji.* Translated by Edward Seidensticker. New York: Alfred A. Knopf, 1976.

Murase, Mieko. *Japanese Art: Selections from the Mary and Jackson Burke Collection.* New York: The Metropolitan Museum of Art, 1975.

National Museum of Modern Art Tokyo, eds. *Nihon shikkō* [Japanese lacquer]. Tokyo: Lacquer Craft Association, 1982.

Noma, Seiroku. *The Arts of Japan. Volume 1: Ancient and Medieval. Volume 2: Late Medieval to Modern.* Translated and adapted by John Rosenfield and Glenn T. Webb. Tokyo & New York: Kodansha International, 1965–66.

Nippon Kōdō. *Kōdō* [The incense ceremony]. Tokyo: Nippon Kōdō, 1982.

Okada, Barbra Teri. *A Sprinkling of Gold: The Lacquer Box Collection of Elaine Ehrenkranz.* Newark: The Newark Museum, 1983.

—— with Mary G. Neill. *Real and Imaginary Beings.* New Haven: Yale University Art Gallery, 1980.

—— and Valrae Reynolds. *Japan: The Enduring Heritage.* Newark: The Newark Museum, 1983.

Okada Jō, Matsuda Gonroku, and Arakawa Hirokazu, eds. *Nihon no shitsugei* [Japanese lacquer arts]. 4 vols. Tokyo: Chūō Kōronsha, 1978–9.

——. *Tōyō shitsugeishi no kenkyū* [Studies in the history of East Asian lacquer arts]. Tokyo: Chūō Kōron Bijutsu Shuppan, 1978.

Okada, Yuzuru. *Japanese Family Crests.* Tokyo: Japanese National Railways, Board of Tourist Industry, 1941.

Papinot, E. *Historical and Geographic Dictionary of Japan.* Yokohama: Kelly and Walsh, 1910.

Pekarik, Andrew. *Japanese Lacquer, 1600–1900: Selections from the Charles A. Greenfield Collection.* New York: The Metropolitan Museum of Art, 1980.

Reim, J. J. *The Industries of Japan.* London: Hodder and Stoughton, 1899.

Rimer and Morrell. *Guide to Japanese Poetry.* Boston: G. K. Hall & Co., 1984.

Rodd, Laurel Rasplica, with Mary Catherine Henkenius, trans. *Kokinshū: A Collection of Poems Ancient and Modern.* Princeton: Princeton University Press, 1984.

Rosenfield, John M. and Shujiro Shimada. *Traditions of Japanese Art: Selections from the Kimiko and John Powers Collection.* Boston: Fogg Art Museum, Harvard University, 1970.

Sansom, George B. *A History of Japan.* 3 vols. Stanford: Stanford University Press, 1958–63.

——. *Japan: A Short Cultural History.* New York: Appleton-Century-Crofts, 1962.

Sawaguchi Goichi. *Nihon shikkō no kenkyū* [Studies in Japanese lacquer]. 2nd edition. Tokyo: Bijutsu Shuppansha, 1966.

Sekai dai hyakka jiten [The world encyclopedia]. Tokyo: Heibonsha, 1965.

Shimizu Yoshiaki, ed. *Japan: The Shaping of Daimyō Culture, 1185–1868.* Washington, D.C.: National Gallery of Art, 1988.

Shively, Donald H. "Sumptuary Regulations and Statutes in Early Tokugawa Japan." *Harvard Journal of Asiatic Studies* 25 (1964–65).

Smith, Lawrence and Victor Harris. *Japanese Decorative Arts from the Seventeenth to the Nineteenth Centuries.* London: British Museum Publications, 1982.

Stern, Harold P. *Birds, Beasts, Blossoms, and Bugs.* New York: Harry N. Abrams, 1976

Suguwara Nobuhiko, et al. *Kindai nihon no shitsugei* [Lacquer Art of Modern Japan]. Tokyo: Tokyo National Museum of Modern Art, 1979.

Suntory Museum of Art. *One Hundred Masterpieces from the Collection of the Suntory Museum of Art.* Tokyo: Suntory Museum of Art, 1981.

Suzuki Norio. "Shikkō (chūsei-hen)" [Lacquerwork (medieval)]. *Nihon no bijutsu,* no. 230 (July 1985).

Takahashi Ken'ichi. *Daimyōke no kamon* [Daimyo family crests]. Tokyo, 1974.

Takeuchi Kyūichi. "Ogawa Haryū ō" [Ogawa Haryū as an old man]. *Shoga kottō zasshi,* no. 90 (December 1915); no. 92 (February 1916); no. 93 (March 1916).

———. "Ritsuō seisaku no kōkeisha" [Inheritors of Ritsuō's craft]. *Shoga kottō zasshi*, no. 96 (June 1916).

Tanizaki Jun'ichiro. *In Praise of Shadows.* Translated by Thomas S. Harper and Edward G. Seidensticker. New Haven: Leete's Island Books, 1977.

Tazawa Yutaka. *Biographical Dictionary of Japanese Art.* New York & Tokyo: Kodansha International, 1981.

Tokyo National Museum. *Textiles and Lacquer.* Pageant of Japanese Art, vol. 5. Tokyo: Tōtō Shuppan, 1958.

———. *Tokubetsuten: Tōyō no shikkōgei* [Special exhibit: lacquer arts of East Asia]. Tokyo, Tokyo National Museum: 1977.

———. *Tōyō no shikkōgei* [Lacquer arts of East Asia]. Tokyo: Benridō, 1978.

———. *Lacquered Furniture: Stationery.* Illustrated Catalogues of the Tokyo National Museum. Tokyo: Tokyo National Museum, 1985.

Tompkins, John Bass, and Dorothy Campbell. *People, Places, and Things in Henri Joly's "Legend in Japanese Art."* Alexandria, Virginia: Kirin Books & Art, 1978.

Ts'ao T'ien Ch'in, Ho Ping-Yo, and Joseph Needham. "An Early Medieval Chinese Alchemical Text." *Ambix* 7:3 (1959)

Urushi kōgei jiten [Dictionary of lacquerware]. Tokyo: Kōgei Shuppansha, 1978.

Urushi Study Group. *Urushi: Proceedings of the Urushi Study Group, June 10–27, 1985, Tokyo.* Edited by N. S. Brommelle and Perry Smith. Marina Del Rey: Getty Conservation Institute, 1988.

Varley, H. Paul. *A Syllabus of Japanese Civilization.* 2nd edition. New York: Columbia University Press, 1968.

———. *Japanese Culture: A Short History.* New York: Praeger, 1973.

Volker, T. *The Animal in Far Eastern Art.* Leiden: E. J. Brill, 1975.

von Ragué, Beatrix. *A History of Japanese Lacquerwork.* Translated by Annie R. de Wasserman. Toronto & Buffalo: University of Toronto Press, 1976.

von Siebold, Dr. P. F. *Manners and Customs of the Japanese in the Nineteenth Century.* 1841. Reprint, Rutland, Vermont & Tokyo: Charles E. Tuttle, 1973.

Wang Shixiang. *Ancient Chinese Lacquer.* Translated by Wang Wenjiong. Beijing: Foreign Languages Press, 1987.

Warner, Langdon. *Japanese Sculpture of the Tempyō Period.* Cambridge: Harvard University Press, 1964.

Watson, Burton, ed. and trans. *The Columbia Book of Chinese Poetry: From Early Times to the Thirteenth Century.* New York: Columbia University Press, 1984.

Watt, James C. Y. and Barbara Brennan Ford. *East Asian Lacquer: The Florence and Herbert Irving Collection.* New York: The Metropolitan Museum of Art, 1991.

Weber, Victor F. *Koji hōten* [Dictionary of Ancient Matters]. 1922, 2 vols. Reprint, New York: Hacker Art Books, 1965.

Weintraub, Steven, Tsujimoto Kanya, and Sadae Walters. "Urushi and Conservation: The Use of Japanese Lacquer in the Restoration of Japanese Art." *Ars Orientalis* 11 (1979).

Wheelwright, Carolyn, ed. *Word in Flower: The Visualization of Classical Literature in Seventeenth-Century Japan.* New Haven: Yale University Art Gallery, 1989.

Williams, C.A.S. *Outlines of Chinese Symbolism and Art Motifs.* New York: Dover, 1976.

Yamane Yūzo. *Sōtatsu to Kōrin* [Sotatsu and Korin]. Nihon no Bijutsu, vol 18. Tokyo: Shōgakkan, 1976.

Yamato Bunkakan. *Shikkō* [Lacquerwork]. Yamato Bunkakan shozōhin zuhan mokuroku, vol. 3. Nara: Yamato Bunkakan, 1975.

Yonemura, Ann. *Japanese Lacquer.* Washington, D.C.: The Freer Gallery of Art, Smithsonian Institute, 1979.

Yoshida, Mitsukuni, ed. *Shikki nyūmon* [Introduction to lacquer]. Kyoto: Tankosha, 1981.

Yoshimura Moto. *Kōdaiji maki-e.* Kyoto: Kyoto National Museum, 1971.

Yoshino Tomio. *Japanese Lacquer Ware.* Tokyo: Japan Travel Bureau, 1959.

Index

The "weathermark" identifies this book as a product of Weatherhill, Inc., publishers of fine books on Asia and the Pacific. Editorial supervision: D.S. Noble. Book design: Liz Trovato. Cover design: Mariana Canelo Francis. Production supervision: Bill Rose. Printed and bound at Oceanic Graphic Press, Hong Kong. The typeface used is Centaur.